PREVIOUS BOOKS

Healing by Contacting Your Cells.
Journal Excerpts from the Ring of Fire.
What Can You Do To Help Our World?
2013 And Beyond.
2013 And Beyond Part II.
2014 World Journals.
2015 World Healing.
2015 World Healing II.
2016 World Journals.

2016

WORLD JOURNALS II

Barbara Wolf and Margaret Anderson

authorHOUSE®

AuthorHouse™
1663 Liberty Drive
Bloomington, IN 47403
www.authorhouse.com
Phone: 1 (800) 839-8640

Published by AuthorHouse 01/17/2017

ISBN: 978-1-5246-5882-3 (sc)
ISBN: 978-1-5246-5880-9 (hc)
ISBN: 978-1-5246-5881-6 (e)

Library of Congress Control Number: 2017900839

Print information available on the last page.

This book is printed on acid-free paper.

Barbara wearing pink sweater and Margaret wearing white sweater.
Photo taken by Salwa Zeidan with city in background of Dubai, United Arab Emirates.

This book is dedicated to Barbara's husband Jack
and to the rest of the world.

ACKNOWLEDGEMENTS

Salwa Zeidan
Jagdish and Bharti Gandhi
Paul Winter
David J. Adams
Carmen Balhestero
Masami Saionji
Hideo Nakazawa
Fumi Johns Stewart
Masaru Emoto
Hiroyoshi Kawagishi
Mitsuru Ooba
Kazuyuki Namatame
Chief Golden Light Eagle
Grandmother SilverStar
Patricia Cota-Robles
Shishir Srivastava
Marco and Irene Hadjidakis
James Twyman
Divino Roberto Verissimo
Yogendra Munankarmy
Peter and Judy Dix
Kim Reid
James Tyberonn
Stella Edmundson
Daniel Petito
Robert Ziefel
Emma Kunz
Judy Moss

FOREWORD

We firmly believe in what we believe, and we realize you may not agree with everything we believe. Probably we would not agree with everything you agree with. But let us put aside our differences and let us be friends.

It's the world that matters. Mother Earth needs help and we are trying to give it to her. That is all that is expected.

CONTENTS

INTRODUCTION

Chapter 1 will take you first to Barbara's exciting journey to the United Arab Emirates and then to India to be a speaker.

Chapter 2 has Margaret's exciting journey to both places and she too is a speaker in India. Our book cover is from a photograph taken by Salwa Zeidan of the United Arab Emirates.

Chapter 3 finds us in The Netherlands to participate in the annual International Day of Peace with Marco and Irene Hadjidakis who, several years ago, helped Barbara plant a peace pole in front of the Peace Palace.

Chapter 4 has us in Philadelphia poking our noses into the origins of the United States of America. We visit Independence Hall where the Declaration of Independence and the Constitution were written.

Chapter 5 is a visit to a Farmington Quaker Meeting where we extend our knowledge of the early principles of the United States.

Chapter 6 tells you about our determination to use the powerful energies of Niagara Falls to help stabilize our continent.

Chapter 7, Onondaga Lake is considered the most poisonous lake in the world. We go there to give positive energies to this place. A sea gull watches us.

Chapter 8, Canandaigua deals with our journey to the lake as well as to the big Veterans Hospital where we give flowers and we are surprised to learn who has received the flowers.

Chapter 9, Energizing Water takes us to several waterways to stimulate the water, and the whales and dolphins help us. This is worldwide work stimulated by David J. Adams of Australia.

Chapter 10, we are in New York City for the Winter Solstice, and we go to the magnificent Cathedral of Saint John the Divine as well as to the fascinating Brooklyn Tabernacle. We loved our travels and we hope you will love to read about them!

CHAPTER 1

United Arab Emirates and India

From Barbara:

November 5, 2016, Joan, our taxi driver, picks us up at the reasonable hour of 9 a.m. and takes us to the airport for a flight to New York City's JFK Airport. We are headed to Dubai in the United Arab Emirates and then to India.

How wonderful to leave at such a COMFORTABLE hour. Usually, Joan drives us to the airport at a very early morning hour. Well, not this time.

We take a Delta flight to JFK and when we land at New York's big airport, our plane cruises slowly along the ground to reach Delta's terminal. During this slow ground cruise, I see a big batch of airplanes parked at a long terminal for the Emirates. I know we will take one of them to Dubai.

When our plane is parked at its gate, we tag along with an assistant who reduces mightily our need to untangle the proper way to reach the Emirates planes. We need to walk here and we need to walk there and then we need to take a bus to another terminal and on and on.

Well, we do reach the Emirates terminal and we do board the proper plane for Dubai and we do settle down in seats 49A and 49B to tolerate twelve hours and fifty minutes flying time.

Actually, the ride is not intolerable. The plane moves along steadily without bumping here and there and the stewardess and two stewards, always with smiles, treat us attentively. Food and drink come steadily throughout the trip.

I watch on TV the progress of our flight.

When we reach Dubai, and this in not the first time I have been here. I am ready for its VERY BIG airport facilities. Two assistants are waiting to guide Margaret and me because my feeling is that this place is so big and so complex, one could get lost for hours.

Well, our assistants solve the 'getting lost' problem, and they, two Filipinos speaking excellent English, guide us easily through the passport checks, the baggage checks, etc, etc. When we leave the last baggage check and we are ready to exit the terminal, we approach a line of men holding signs with the names of passengers. And yes, sure enough, I see my name with Margaret's name on one of the signs. Good! This man will drive us to our hotel. It has been prearranged.

We will be taken to the Wyndham Dubai Marina Hotel which is only a couple blocks from the Persian Gulf.

The Persian Gulf, after all, is a main reason for stopping at Dubai rather than going directly to India where Margaret and I will be speakers at a big conference. The water of the Gulf needs help. It is part of a big water system that needs help. The Arabian Sea to the Gulf of Oman to the Persian Gulf to the Tigris River and the Euphrates River which reach to the center of Turkey.

How many centuries have these waterways been used by humanity? The water cannot speak. Is the use always a good one? No thoughts of aggression? Only peace thoughts?

Margaret and I will send loving thoughts to the waterways!

As the driver is taking us to the Wyndham Dubai Marina Hotel, I look out the car windows at Dubai. I think my first time visiting the city was in 2007, and about five times since then.

In the 'old days', the city was small. Today? VERY LARGE AND GROWING MOMENT BY MOMENT. I look at the expressway we are using to reach the hotel. A first class expressway. Many cars are using it, and most cars look new. The newspaper called Gulf News says by 2019, three years from now, there will be self-driving vehicles. Also, in the near future, Dubai will have hydrogen-powered taxis that can go 500 kilometers without needing to be refueled. The refueling can take only minutes, which, according to the Gulf News, is better than electric cars that take longer to recharge.

Yes, Dubai has gone a long way since I first visited this place in 2007. I am looking at VERY TALL, thin skyscrapers. What businesses are located in these VERY TALL, thin skyscrapers? I think they are worldwide businesses and so probably there are people from around the world who go there.

In 2002, Dubai Healthcare City (DHCC) was started to give high quality, free healthcare to those living in Dubai as well as those living around the world. Over one million people visit yearly, and the number continues to increase. There are more than 120 medical facilities including a number of hospitals as well as more than 4,000 licensed professionals.

Yes, Dubai is an incredible place to visit. And, there are many hotels to hold those who come here, for whatever reason.

When our driver reaches the Wyndham Dubai Marina Hotel, helpful hotel crew take our bags to the front desk and we are given an already-assigned room on the twenty-second floor. A look out the window shows us a piece of the Persian Gulf. Not a full length as I had expected, but never mind. Tomorrow morning our friend Salwa Zeidan will come with her driver to take us wherever we want to go.

She is the owner of an art gallery who lives 'down the road' from Dubai in a city called Abu Dhabi, and we are anxious to see her. We remain good friends even though we live 'on the other side of the world'.

I first met her a bit over ten years ago when I was a speaker in Istanbul. Salwa and her son were sitting across from me at a big table when we were dinner guests (with about forty others) of Mevlana, head of The World Brotherhood Union, author of The Knowledge Book.

We, Salwa and her son, became friends and from this first meeting with each other, we became such good friends that I went with two others to Abu Dhabi to meet Salwa and lecture at four female universities. The arrangements were made by her close friend, the sheikh in charge of education. Especially female education. This was an incredible experience! The sheikh not only arranged the lectures, but transportation and everything else. We even briefly met him.

In any case, the United Arab Emirates is not a strange place for me. I like this place.

————————

It is now November 7, a bit before noon, and Salwa is at the hotel with her driver to take us to the waters of the Persian Gulf. Margaret has Vortex Symbols ready to put into the water.*

*See Glossary: Vortex Symbols.

The driver is a Filipino who can speak English, and so we can speak to him. He takes us past Burj Al Arab, Tower of the Arabs, which looks like an extraordinarily tall sail. The sheikh who arranged for us lectures at four female universities a few years ago booked a free night at a fancy hotel near Burj Al Arab, a tall artificial sail where one can take an elevator up the interior to have coffee, tea, a meal, etc.

Well, now the Filipino driver is driving us beyond this unusual sail place and Salwa is now speaking with someone via an iPod in her hand. She is asking for the name of a place of a restaurant where we can have a fish lunch. Yes! There is a nearby place, and our Filipino driver stops here almost immediately. It is a small place with an outside dining area, and we seat ourselves outside with others who are mainly male. They look like fisherman. Well, maybe.

In any case, Salwa selects a fish with the restaurant owner, and while it is cooking, we go with her to walk on a pier that takes us a bit away from the shore. As we are walking on the pier, we give LOVE to the water, from 'top to bottom' -- from the Arabian Sea to the Gulf of Oman to the Persian Gulf to the Tigris River and the Euphrates River.

With her iPod, Salwa takes a photograph of us standing on the pier at the water, and she sends it to Margaret's computer in the U.S.A. This photograph with its wonderful memories waits for us to return.

We now join our Filipino driver at the small restaurant to eat outside the fish that has been cooking since we walked to the water and the pier. IT IS DELICIOUS!

After lunch, our only thought is for the Filipino driver to take us to a beach where Margaret can draw Vortexes at the water's edge. When we do reach a beach, it is a wide one, very wide, and it is packed with white sand. Beautiful!

Few people are on the beach and no vehicles except one van that looks like a Security van. We want to park our car on the beach so Margaret will not need to walk far to the shoreline, but, are we to drive on the beach? Tire tracks on the packed white sand tell us that others have driven on the beach. Well, the Security van makes a decision for us. It begins to move down the beach and in a few moments, there is no van to say 'no' to us if we park on the beach.

We do this and Margaret takes the Vortexes down a slope to the water's edge. We cannot see her but we know she has reached her destination.

And then the Security van returns and stops beside us! Oh! Oh! He rolls down his window and says something to me in Arabic. In English, I give him a reply that I do not understand him, and Salwa gets out of the car and begins talking to him in Arabic in a friendly manner. He listens patiently and makes a remark or two and she continues talking to him in a friendly manner. From the car, I watch, and I know that this Security man has decided to let matters run their own way. We can stay parked on the beach. Salwa has pointed to where Margaret is putting down the Vortexes, and even though I cannot understand the Arabic language, I see that he is not negative.

When Margaret finishes, reappears and gets into the car, Salwa gets in, too, and our Filipino driver begins to slowly move the car toward the road and off the beach. I sit closest to the Security man and he gives us a short wave. One wave, as I know is common here. Well, I give him my common custom -- a smile and quick waves back and forth without stopping. He sees this and with a smile, he begins imitating me -- short waves back and forth.

What fun!

_____

And now it is time to return to our hotel and say goodbye to Salwa and her driver. We tell Salwa we will wait for her photographs to reach home.

INDIA

November 8 arrives and it is time to fly from Dubai to Delhi, capitol of India. Or, is it officially called New Delhi? When we are in the capital, we see road signs using both names.

Our Emirates flight from Dubai leaves at 10 a.m., and so, to be certain there is no delay from our hotel to the airport, we leave at 6 a.m. via a hotel shuttle. At this hour, we feel there will be few cars on the road to make delays, and we are right. Within a half hour, we are at the airport.

And now, how do we find the correct departure gate? We are taken to Terminal 3, and it is HUGE. Fortunately, some airport workers are already working at this early hour, and they direct us to the correct bus to take us to our gate.

Yes, I think the Emirates is the biggest airline company in the world. When one sees a global map of red lines showing where they fly, it is mind-boggling.

Well, today we are taking a relatively small plane to Delhi. Our seats are 27A and 27C with no one sitting at 27B until the last moment before departure when a heavy-set Indian woman sits down. She speaks English, as do many Indians, and we are soon talking with her. She tells us that it is the time of Diwali, an important festival of lights to celebrate yearly a victory of light over darkness and good over evil. Millions of lights are shown on house roofs and buildings, and there is the traditional burning of fires for five days. This year, she says, the burning of fires has created air pollution so severe, schools have been closed for three days.

Margaret suggests that fires should not be allowed, and the woman immediately dismisses this, saying the burning is a tradition. I realize that if Margaret had suggested to someone that the Christmas holiday should not be allowed, there would be the same negative reaction.

In any case, Margaret and I know now that Delhi will be heavily polluted. We do not tell the hefty woman sitting with us that one of the main reasons for stopping there is to judge the extent of air pollution. A few years ago, when we were in Delhi, the pollution was, in our opinion, extreme. We saw homeless people sitting on curbs and some males using trees as toilets, and we wondered then how the homeless can exist day and night with such pollution. Now, it is worse. When we are landing, we see no normal blue sky. Only black.

How can a child survive who is born here with a breathing problem?

In any case, when we land at Delhi, we are assisted by two airport workers of Bangladeshi origin. One of them speaks very good English, and we are telling him that a few years ago in New York City we listened to Muhammad Yunus, a Bangladeshi, who was the first to conceive of microfinancing and he put it to work for the ordinary Bangladeshi. This concept spread rapidly and enthusiastically, and Muhammad Yunus was awarded a Nobel Peace Prize.

It puzzles me that the two Bangladeshi working at the Delhi Airport do not seem to understand what I am saying. Here they are, working a great number of miles from their homeland because they need money and the airplane companies need English-speaking workers to accommodate those who are flying. English tends to be a common language.

But, if the two Bangladeshi working at the Delhi Airport had stayed home and entered the microfinancing system of getting money, wouldn't that be an easier way to live?

Well, the two at the airport are a big help to Margaret and me. When we manage to end the traditional system of passport control, baggage acknowledgement, etc., and we are ready to find a shuttle person holding a sign with our names, there is no shuttle person holding a sign with our names.

WHAT ARE WE TO DO?????

One Bangladeshi knows exactly what to do. Immediately, he uses his cell phone to call the hotel, and within five minutes he has an answer. The shuttle person has been delayed while making his way to the airport and so Margaret and I should wait.

We wait less than five minutes and the shuttle driver arrives. HURRAY!!! That problem is quickly solved.

We say good-bye to the two Bangladeshi and we climb into the shuttle car to go to the WelcomHotel Dwarka about a half hour from the airport.

And yes, before we arrive, we realize that Dwarka is probably the name of a suburb of Delhi. Undoubtedly, this is the reason why the word Dwarka is attached to the hotel's name.

Well, the WelcomHotel Dwarka is, in my opinion, a FIRST CLASS hotel. WOW! And it is not all that expensive. Again, we booked this hotel through <u>Hotels.com</u>.

Inside, we look at a large dining room, and we learn there are set times for eating a buffet-style breakfast, lunch, and dinner. However, if we want to eat at a time different from the buffet-presented meal times, we can also do that. Chefs are always on duty to cook for us.

We are hungry and the buffet-style meals have not yet begun. However, a smiling dining room hostess tells us to sit down anyway and the chefs will cook what we want.

We tell her we write books and in our next book we want to include the hotel's name and her name because she and the hotel are being so gracious. She points to her nametag that has the name of Nancy and we are surprised. How can an Indian woman have a common American name? It is her grandmother's name, she says. She has been named after her grandmother. Well, all of this is a surprise.

We have a delicious meal in the big dining room with only ourselves eating and then we decide to go outside the hotel to sit at a pool built to entertain swimmers and those who want to sit on chairs at the water.

As for Margaret and me, once we are at the pool, will air pollution drive us inside the hotel again?

Yes.

No one is at this beautiful outside place, and we think that pollution has put a 'no' stamp on thoughts of being there. We stay a few minutes and return to the hotel interior.

As a substitute for siting at the pool, we discuss whether or not we should hire someone to drive us on a quick tour of Delhi. We know this city. It is not a stranger to us, but.............

We go to the front desk to ask about making a short afternoon tour of Delhi. Well, the reply is not encouraging. One has to make plans in advance.

And also, we ask ourselves, do we really want to leave the hotel and breathe pollution? No. So, we decide to watch on television comments about the U.S.A. election that has just happened. A woman running for the Presidential office has received 2 million votes more than her opponent and yet she has lost the race. Is this a custom throughout the world?

———————

November 10, 2:10 p.m. we are aboard a Jet Airways flight to Lucknow, India, our ultimate destination for this journey to the United Arab Emirates and India and we have something in our pockets that we do not expect to have. The Indian rupees we bought at the hotel in Delhi. Less than twenty-four hours after we buy them, we turn them in for dollars at the front desk where we bought them. And, guess what -- our desire is rejected. The rupees cannot be returned for dollars. The Indian government has put a 'hold' on changing rupee currency.

WHAT?????????????????!!!!!!!!

How can a government that has been operating days, weeks, months, years and years and years and years, suddenly say that rupees cannot be exchanged for other money?

We just bought the rupees YESTERDAY!!!!!

Well, apparently there has been counterfeit or something like that going on and so the government has put down a hammer saying STOP. No more exchange of money.

At the airport, we try to change the money. No. Later, when we return to the U.S.A., we try at airports. No. We try at banks. No.

WOW!

Well, we need to change our negative reaction to the positive. The experience gives us an understanding of how millions are feeling just now that they have no good money. We only lost a little money, seventy dollars exchanged for rupees. Others may have lost EVERYTHING. The rupees we have will forever remind us of what has happened.

———————

Why is it that Margaret and I are just now coming to Lucknow, India?

Yearly, at this time of year, the City Montessori School in Lucknow, has a world meeting at the school. This is the largest school in the world -- around 55,000 students. It was founded by Dr. Jagdish Gandhi and his wife Mrs. Bharti Gandhi who sat years ago on a sidewalk teaching five students. And now, look at what has happened -- five students have turned into nearly 55,000 students. In 2002, the UNESCO Prize for Peace Education was awarded to the school.*

*See Glossary: City Montessori School.

The Gandhis believe that the goal of education is to bring children to a point where they are not only intelligent, but they should be taught to be good and the pride of the human race, a citizen of the world. Schools should be the lighthouses of society.

From November 9 through 15, the CMS in Lucknow will become the site of the 17th International Conference of the Chief Justices of the World.

*See Glossary: 17th International Conference of Chief Justices.

The main topic is the discussion of Article 51 of the Constitution of India which promotes international peace and security, maintains just and honorable relations between nations, fosters respect for international law and treaty obligations in the dealings of organized peoples with one another, and encourages settlement of international disputes by arbitration.

To promote success for the above is concentrated on the building of a World Parliament that would be strong enough to promote international laws applying to all countries of the world. In other words, the uniting of all countries as One.

Well, a great number of Chief Justices of the world have said they will come to Lucknow, India, in November to work on the progress of Article 51, and Margaret and I will be there to 'look at' the progress.

Additionally, we have been asked to speak and I have chosen the topic of the Rights of Children and Margaret has chosen the topic of the Rights of Women.

Here is the talk I gave at Lucknow:

Over the years I have been watching attempts to form a world government so all will become equal and the world will be come peaceful.

I was especially interested when several years ago CMS students collected nearly 100,000 signatures requesting that former Secretary General of the United Nations Dr. Kofi A. Annan take steps to form a world government to insure world peace rather than the world continuing to fight.

Kofi Annan replied to the CMS students who collected the 100,000 signatures. He said a Millennium Summit was formed but the purpose of forming a world government failed because those who came to the summit preferred to speak about problems in their own countries rather than speak about the formation of an international system that would address all the world nations and its people.

As for myself, I continue to admire the great concentrated efforts of students who collected 100,000 signatures. My thought is that the students themselves should be taught how to bring world order. Easy communication via the computer can bring instant communication between a student in India and a student living in the United Kingdom. The world of students can become friends with each other.

Margaret Anderson and I have written a book called What Can You Do To Help Our World? It has been translated into Hindi. This book gives close to 100 suggestions that can stimulate the minds of children into thinking globally. We give names, addressees, and websites. For example, we give information about an extremely active organization called Global Youth Action Network. Youth in every continent are active in this organization. While writing this paper, I spoke on the phone with a representative who said there are 700,000 members throughout the world.

Yes, the book has telephone numbers, email addresses, websites, street addresses. This brings together youth from India, South Africa, United States, Nigeria, Afghanistan, Turkey, etc.

My talk included the comment that I have visited CMS for over ten years. When I pass a youth, I smile, shake hands and say a few words. My thought is that these children will remember a foreigner stopping to shake hands. When the youth reach the age of twenty-one and they have become grown adults meeting others throughout the world, they will remember the smiles and handshakes coming from their childhood. They will react positively, warmly, to the adults they are now meeting. Some youth will take jobs of a high level for their country. Their hearts need to be positive hearts to help our world. There is hope that some day they may actually be involved in forming a government that includes the entire world.

——————————

This year when we fly from Delhi to Lucknow for the conference, on arrival we do not ask for assistance. Even though the Lucknow terminal seems to continually be enlarged and now is extensively enlarged since the first time I arrived nearly twenty years ago, Margaret and I easily follow others to the exit where we expect to be met by one of the conference's head officials who has emailed us saying he would be at the terminal personally to greet us.

Well, at the exit, no one comes forward to greet us. What do we do now?

We walk just a bit to the place where, over the course of years, we have been given an official greeting as conference attendees. This greeting includes a large garland of orange flowers put around our necks and we are photographed.

And yes, we easily find this place, and uniformed school children are saying to us "Welcome to India" as we walk past them. But, where is someone to put us through the custom of a welcome with flowers?

Then, as we are standing at the welcome place, a man comes rushing to us saying he has been trying to find us. The official who should be here is not here because he is delayed by a problem with the big bell.

Actually, we understand about the big bell because it was at the last conference we attended. It was brought to the foot of the big auditorium stage so that its candles can be lighted, and then the bell for PEACE is struck.

Now it is the time of Diwali, a Hindu festival of lights celebrated every year in India. Yes, the conference we will be attending has perfect timing.

Well, we have received no garlands when we arrive in Lucknow, but we are put into a car and driven a short way to the center of Lucknow and to the buildings of the City Montessori School, our residence until we leave Lucknow.

We are given a room at the International Guest House, third floor, or, two stops if we take the elevator that is beside our room. This is a two-bed apartment with a bathroom, and we are delighted to throw down our bags and rest a few minutes before heading to a place we think meals are normally reserved for teachers and other school workers. We are hungry and we hope this place is open!

Yes, it is open but empty except for one man sitting at a table and another man getting food from a variety of offerings on a white-clothed table extending thirty or more feet.

I ask the man sitting at a table -- can Margaret and I eat with you? Yes.

And that is how we meet Divino Roberto Verissimo of Brazil and Yogendra Munankarmy of Nepal. They are attending the conference and they are sharing lodging. Both will be speakers.

––––––––––––

November 11, it is quiet when we wake in the morning, and we have survived an interesting experience around midnight. Suddenly, very loud, and I mean LOUD MUSIC, begins. Even covering the ears with blankets will not remove the noise. We phone 'downstairs' to ask what is happening, and we are told that this is a celebration for a marriage. We are to wait about ten minutes and the music will stop. Well, it was a LONG ten minutes. More like a half hour.

In the morning I decide that if the marriage music celebration happens again, I need to be prepared ahead of time to program my mind that I will remain asleep. And yes, I do that and there is more marriage music but I do not hear it. I remain sleeping.

Yesterday we have seen the Chief Justices of the world arriving. How many are there? MANY. 200 plus. Some with their wives. Where are they from? I think sixty countries. They have been sightseeing in Delhi and other places for a couple days before the conference begins. A few years ago, when I began attending the conference, I went sightseeing, but this time, no. To satisfy one's self, one does not need to go to the same place over and over again.

Now, on the steps of a big auditorium, Margaret and I sit with the Chief Justices to have our pictures taken. I sit in the second row with a young man who introduces himself as Dr. Gandhi's grandson, and we speak a bit. A big garland of flowers is put around my neck as well as a lengthy, elaborate, colorful scarf, and a big plastic world globe is put in my hands.

Then we are all photographed.

When the photographs are finished, Dr. Gandhi's grandson is asked to speak a few words. Just before that, he has told me he had not been a part of the earlier world conferences because he was attending a school not close to this place. I think he was in England. My feeling is that now that his schooling is over, he will be more involved with these yearly conferences.

After the photographing, students perform on stage inside the auditorium by formally addressing each other according to the United Nations custom of representatives of nations addressing each other.

When Margaret and I enter the auditorium to watch, we are a bit confused about where we should be sitting. Then we realize we should look for our names posted on the seats. Also indicating our seating are posted two tiny U.S.A. flags. How many from the U.S.A. are attending? We see only two names. For us, this is amazing because the world is well represented today by France, Egypt, Zambia, Croatia, Mauritius, Sudan, Zimbabwe, Philippines, Madagascar, Slovenia, Argentina, Peru, Ecuador, Benin, Poland, South Africa, Costa Rica, Cameroon, Lebanon, Nicaragua, India, etc.

Tonight, meals are poolside, and we have been waiting for this! Behind the long string of buildings pertaining to the school is a big blue pool, and when there will be poolside eating, BIG SPRAYS OF WATER SHOOT STRAIGHT UP TWENTY FEET OR MORE.

Our two new friends, one from Brazil and the other from Nepal, are eating and we join them.

Yes, it has been a big, wonderful day.

———————

December 9, afternoon:

When I return home and I am writing the India experiences for the book you are reading, we have had an exciting email from Dr. Gandhi inviting us to the next conference. We had just written to him about our reaction to the International Conference and we said we were extremely pleased to attend because the conference was so lively with wonderful speeches giving proposals for the children and the world.

I said we would be speaking on Brazil television about the conference and this television organization will send it around the world.

I told Dr. Gandhi we have see CMS students being schooled in a professional manner so that this would result in some of them being capable of having jobs at such a high level that they would become effectively involved in reaching the current goal -- honorable relationship between nations, respect for international law, settlement by arbitration of international disputes. I thanked him for his tireless efforts in helping the world.

Dr. Gandhi's email reply contained over thirty email addresses that would be receiving my email and his reply. These addresses included every top official associated with the school.

Margaret has written also about our participation in the India conference and now you will hear from her. But first she will write you about experiences in the United Arab Emirates.

======================================

CHAPTER 2

United Arab Emirates and India

From Margaret:

November 5:

This morning, Joan the taxi driver takes us to the airport for our Delta plane which begins our journey to the United Arab Emirates and India. Our first flight takes us to JFK Airport, and when we begin flying, there are many clouds and then it clears. I look down and see especially beautiful trees with autumn leaves.

At JFK, while waiting for our next flight which will be an Emirates flight to Dubai, we sit with a young male pharmacist from the Philippines who is flying to Abu Dhabi. We have a long wait here and we enjoy speaking with him. Our Emirates plane leaves at 4:35 p.m. and is a double-decker plane stuffed with people. Luckily, we have an empty seat between us.

When the huge plane begins moving, it is so smooth I am not sure we are already in the air. During the flight, the stewardesses are efficient and work hard serving drinks and delicious food. The film programs are excellent. I especially liked horse racing in Dubai and Queen Elizabeth at 90.

November 6:

We arrive Dubai at 1:45 p.m., and I am amazed to be at one of the largest airports in the world. We are assisted through passport control, then Security, and then to a shuttle to take us to our hotel, the Wyndham Dubai Marina. Here we are given a beautiful room on floor 22 with a view of the marina, and I know that the waters of this marina go out to the Gulf. We will see the Persian Gulf tomorrow. I feel very comfortable in this room.

Later, we have an exquisite dinner with fresh mint tea.

———————

November 7:

I am writing my journal notes early in the morning and I am thinking about the drive from the airport to the hotel. There is a feeling of vastness here in Dubai. Everything is so big, so grand, so extreme in size with glitter, chrome and glass, mirrors and reflections. Everything seems new and under construction. The traffic is slow, like rush hour all day.

I see new buildings going higher and higher. It does not feel that anyone lives near the ground. I feel surrounded by visions of shopping and amusements for the delight of foreigners. We are beginning to meet people from elsewhere -- Bangladesh, Sri Lanka, Ghana. Everyone is young and enthusiastic.

I feel I am far up in the air. I need to feel grounded. Are people really living in these nearby tall buildings? There is glitter and glass and tallness but this does not quench my desire for a connection to the land. Where is the connection to the land? I am missing the land. Where is the desert? Where are the hawks, the horses, the tents, the ancient buildings that hug the land?

I am listening to thoughts coming from the land:

Centering in Love is the core issue. The whole place here is based on sand – billions and billions of tiny sand particles holding the history of the earth.

Relax, take the long view. The sands shift and yet are always present. We, the sand, hold the memories together. Your mind may scatter but we hold true to Mother Earth, our planet.

The Angels and the prophets and the elements are here close to the surface. This land, this land people, sea people, are always connected to the Stars.

Break out of the buildings and join the sand and stars. Sit by a campfire in the desert and bless the wonders of creation that continue and change evermore. The wise ones, the ancient ones come when the mind stills.

———————

I feel drawn to be outside under the stars by the fire. I feel the Arab and the Native American are one under the stars, outside, beside the fire.

In my hand, I ring a tiny Oshima bell to send out the Love frequency. I bring out the Symbols and Vortexes for planetary healing.

I love you, Mother Earth.
I love you, Mother Earth.

———————

At 6:00 a.m. Barbara tells me that Dubai is a great healing center of the world. Efforts are being made to provide healing facilities to care for millions who are coming from across the world.

Who are the people living here? When I was here earlier, I found them to be quick-witted, sharp, intelligent, good-natured people.

Before noon, our UAE friend Salwa Zeidan comes with her driver to take us to the beach and the water. First though, he drives us to the Jumeirah area with the impressive Tower of the Arabs (Burj Al Arab) building that we visited a few years ago.

Then we stop at a delicious local fish restaurant called Bu Qtair, a favorite place packed with local customers. Salwa orders a fish for us to eat and while it is cooking, we walk to the nearby marina to see the water. She takes our picture which will become the cover of our book.

When we are returning to the restaurant, a large crow stands on a tall pole and announces its presence. The Bird Kingdom and Animal Kingdom are here.

At the restaurant, we enjoy the fish and then our driver takes us to a beach so I can draw the Vortexes for healing the water of the Persian Gulf.

When we arrive, we drive on a sandy beach and I leave the car to walk to the water. The water is delightfully warm and I feel I am one with the water. I use a beach shell to begin drawing the Vortex Symbols in the sand below the waves. The waves break immediately and take each Symbol.

As I draw the Symbols, I speak their names and the names of the Symbols and Vortexes. And I am thinking of healing the waters going up the Persian Gulf to the Tigress and Euphrates Rivers – powerful energy fields of early civilizations. Also, I am sending healing energy for the entire region.

I thank the Guardians of the land and of the sea for allowing me to give these gifts, for accepting these gifts. I thank the shell for helping to do the drawing.

Now I return to the car and I see Barbara and Salwa talking to a Security man. I smile and wave to him and he smiles and waves back.

Later in the evening, in the room, I draw again the full set of Vortex Symbols and I focus on each one. I am giving healing energy to the entire region. May Peace Prevail on Earth.

At the end, I ring the small Oshima bell for closure.

It has been a very moving day.

INDIA

November 8:

To be ready for our 10:00 a.m. flight to Delhi, we leave the hotel early for the airport. On the plane, we have a seatmate, an Indian lady from Albany, New York, who tells us of terrible pollution in Delhi because of Diwali, the Hindu Festival of Lights. Schools are closed because of the pollution from firecrackers. If this is such a health risk, I ask, could the people reduce or stop the use of firecrackers until the pollution is lessened? No, the lady answers. They can't stop the fire works because it is tradition!

When we reach Delhi, we see terrible pollution in the city. A smog hangs over the landscape and the air is charcoal grey. There is no sunlight. One young Indian woman has brought a strong facemask to wear but she finds it too hard to breath when wearing it. Oh my. Everyone is suffering.

On arrival at the Delhi airport, we are shuttled about a half hour to our hotel, the WelcomHotel Dwarka. We see its beautiful architecture of excellent design with strong solid colors. Inside, there are white walls, marble surfaces, mirrors and glass emphasizing light.

Our room on the sixth floor is quite big with a tall ceiling and fine attention to detail. It is modern and comfortable and has air-conditioning.

We take a nap and then we have a delicious dinner.

––––––––––––

November 9:

I wake remembering my delight of Indian textiles – delicate rainbows of patterns -- each woman's sari bright in beauty and color.

At the hotel, I find genuine goodwill coming from the staff. Everyone wants to be of service.

Then I think of the pollution here and the suffering of the tigers and the elephants and other animals. I think of the birds. How can the birds survive here in this highly polluted region?

I bring out the Vortexes and give them to Delhi and all of India.

Now, I am entering a blended meditation thinking about the environment:

There is a lot of sweeping of the streets but what is needed is diminishing of the source of the pollution – coal energy and polluting vehicles. Broom sweeping cannot clean the air. There needs to be a big policy change.

The masses of people weigh down heavily on Nature -- the trees, the animals, the rivers. Let the air be clear so the birds may fly and raise their young. All life forms, the birds and the humans, are now in the same environmental cage.

Health, mental health, physical health are linked hand and hand. All are interrelated. The air affects the lungs, affects the blood, affects the brains. There is a need to reduce the particulate matter in the air. One cannot live inside a smoke stack.

––––––––––––

During the night, I wake worried about India. I have seen the terrible pollution. Now the money system is broken. Yes, I worry about the people. I ask Mother Mary for a message.

Mary's response: Hold to the rope of Love. It anchors, ties the ship to the solid understanding that there is a great order in the chaos you perceive. The realms, the spheres, all move by Love in divine order. Diminish grief. Stand up and embrace Life. That is your precious gift.

My dear, we in the Spiritual World support the humans on the planet today. Lift the mind out of confusion and see the splendor in each sight, each being, each mission. The people gathered here are dedicated to the children. May their lives be lived in a God-given way of Love, hope and growth. Look to each other and see and give my Love to the people. No degrees needed here. No awards. No titles. Just give and receive Love. All wars would cease. All pain would cease. Just Light. Just Love. The heart knows the way.

My blessings, my child. Mary

————————

In the morning, we are up and dressed and have breakfast in the adjacent building. Here we meet two conference attendees who fast become our new friends -- Yogendra Munankarmy from Nepal and the other is Divino Roberto Verissimo of Brazil.

At 10:00 a.m., when the Chief Justices officially arrive from the airport, they are welcomed by the young students, and we are also welcomed. The students are wearing beautiful costumes and carrying the flags of the delegates. 355 attendees are here from 63 countries!!

Our friend of many years Shishir Srivastava comes and takes Barbara and me up the elevator to the delegates' reception area and who is there? Dr. Gandhi! He welcomes us.

Now it is time to have our pictures taken with the Chief Justices on a lengthy flight of stairs to the entrance of the auditorium. Barbara sits in the second row next to Dr. Gandhi's grandson and I am in the next row up. The main photographer is the photographer of India's Prime Minister.

Wow! Many photographers are here taking pictures of the assembled delegates.

Afterward, we enter the auditorium and Shishir helps us find a desk with our name plaques and U.S.A. flags. We watch the morning session of a model United Nations meeting conducted by the older students. They are excellent in their presentation with great clarity of speaking.

On our way to lunch, we meet Mrs. Gandhi and she greets us warmly, calling us her darlings.

We have lunch and then rest in the afternoon.

That evening there is an amazing performance of CMS students and it is delightful to see the school children with their vibrant costumes performing complex choreography – each showing themes of different aspects of diversity, peace and harmony.

At a poolside dinner, we eat with young people from Taiwan, members of the Federation of World Peace and Love. For their television, Barbara and I are interviewed about the conference.

At the dinner table we meet CMS faculty member Mrs. Farida Vahedi who is in charge of youth empowerment. I speak with her about wanting to link her with Carmen Balhestero of Brazil who is interested in expanding educational programs for young people.

A young martial artist from Taiwan is eating with us and he says how important the discipline of martial arts is for him. He beams with enthusiasm.

––––––––––––––

November 12:

The morning begins with a World Unity March and then the ringing of the Peace Bell from Taiwan. Now begins a full day of talks in the auditorium and in classrooms. Universal themes are presented. The speakers may be from different countries and of different ages, but their vision is the same --oneness and inclusiveness, unity of the world through world law, gender equality, protection of the children against harm in war, natural disasters, climate change.

This vision taught by Dr. and Mrs. Gandhi at City Montessori School is to see the whole world as family. With this concept, they believe all international disputes could be solved without conflict and the world would be one.

We have lunch with a Chief Justice from Kampala, Uganda, and he invites us to visit him.

A grand dinner in the evening is held at the mansion of the Governor of Uttar Pradesh and we eat there while a Taiwan group is dancing. We love watching their beautiful performance.

————————

November 13:

The conference continues with an emphasis on the need for the children to have a good life while growing up. They are taught that early conflict begins in the minds of man. Critical is to remove ignorance. One must have a basic awareness and respect for differences. Each person has the right of dignity, equality, and the right of belief. Focus needs to be on justice and liberty for all. Then there will be peace in the world.

In the morning, I sit with a judge from East Timor and we review her talk. She is pleased that I like it. We give her our last book, 2016 World Journals.

In the afternoon, Barbara and I will speak at the session on Human Rights — the Rights of Children, the Rights of Women and Gender Equality. Seven speakers are on our panel and Mrs. Abha Anant, CMS Principal, is moderator. She is excellent and assists with the flow of the session. It moves along smoothly with very good questions from the students.

Barbara and I are filmed while we are speaking and we feel relaxed. Every Thursday we speak on PAX TV Brazil and this has brought comfort to speaking.

Here is my talk given today:

In my country, the U.S.A,. the Rights of Children, Rights of Women and Gender Equality have been heavily influenced by early Quakers who settled in the country over three hundred years ago. Many came from Great Britain in the mid 17th century because they were persecuted. William Penn, a Quaker, in 1681 founded Pennsylvania as a society of equality with freedom of belief for all. Eventually, Quakers spread to Massachusetts, New York State, Ohio, Maryland, Virginia and so forth.

The Quaker experience with persecution made them truly understand the need for gender and political and racial equality. They believed in the dignity of all people.

When Native American people, the Senecas, were in danger of loosing their homeland by being moved beyond the Mississippi River in the middle of the country, the Senecas appealed to the Quakers for help. Immediately, with petitions, letters and pamphlets, the Quakers campaigned strongly for the Senecas and the movement was canceled. Today the Senecas still live on their land.

The Quakers also campaigned for women to have the right to vote. A great number of Quakers attended the first women's rights convention in the year 1848. It took until 1919 for the US Congress to pass an Amendment granting women the right to vote. Now we are in the election of 2016 and we have the possibility of a first woman President.

My desire is that those who are seeking world peace and harmony should look into the background of Quakers to examine their method of helping to establish justice, equality and peace among all people.

Today there remains a serious problem for many women needing to go to water sources and then return home. Their children often go with them. This means these children are not being schooled. They do not learn to read and write. When they are adults, this ignorance may hinder job possibilities.

I am waiting for the time when women and children can raise their consciousness above the need for water and other matters so they can begin to understand the need for a common type of living throughout the world. Living with unity, harmony, and peace.

————————

At the end of my talk, I add how important this Chief Justice conference is for the CMS students who can make a difference in the future because of their education. I put forward a suggestion that there should be a video of the whole session or highlights of the conference that could be put on YouTube so the public could see what is being done here in Lucknow for the children of the world.

————————

November 14:

We have breakfast with our two friends from Nepal and Brazil and we give our book to each of them. After breakfast, Barbara helps Brazilian Divino Roberto speak his lecture in English. In the afternoon, we go to his session and CMS provides a computer man so there can be a translation for him of the students' questions. His talk is successful and the session goes very well. Afterward, the Taiwan group listening to him embraces him and celebrates his talk.

At 9:30 p.m., we are taken to the airport to be ready for our November 15, 1:20 a.m. flight to Dubai. We will arrive Dubai at 4:15 a.m. where we will transfer to an Emirates flight to New York City. On the flight, a wonderful Romanian stewardess who lives in Dubai talks with us. She loves what we do and we give her two E-books.

The trip passes delightfully and when we land in New York City, we transfer to JetBlue and fly home.

Wow. What an amazing trip we have had!

================================

CHAPTER 3

The Netherlands

Joint Journals:

First from Barbara:

Every year, usually September 21, there is an observance called the International Day of Peace at the Peace Palace located at The Hague, The Netherlands. What is the function of the Peace Palace? The United Nations has arranged that this institute in The Netherlands should be the place where countries in conflict with each other meet to resolve problems. We feel an urge to be there on September 21. As we all know, Europe is having a tough time just now because of violence between Muslims and non-Muslims. But this violence is not necessarily a conflict between countries. Would it be settled in the Peace Palace?

I used to live in Paris and in Spain and a few other European places. Then, the atmosphere was calm. It bothers me now when I read of violence.

I have heard nothing about violence in The Netherlands. Good! Our journey now to The Netherlands will give me an opportunity to confirm whether the atmosphere feels calm.

At 12 noon on September 18, Joan, our taxi woman, arrives to take us to the airport. As usual, we have a pleasant talk with her. We already have our boarding passes and so, once we are at the airport, we show them and our passports to Security. We are then allowed to sit at the gate to wait for our plane.

It is warm while we are waiting, with the usual sunshine. Whoever is in charge of the weather has forgotten that winter is approaching and we are happy about that!

When our plane is ready for us, we board and head toward Newark, New Jersey, where we change planes to fly to Schiphol Airport at the edge of Amsterdam. Even though this is an overnight flight, it is an easy one, a pleasant one. No crying babies, no restless passengers. And yes, the plane is smooth enough. It does not jump all over the place. We arrive the next day at 7:45 a.m.

Our friend Marco has emailed he will meet us on arrival and we are worried to have him get out of bed early. The Hague, where he and his wife Irene live, is a bit over an hour's drive to the airport. Well, never mind. Marco is waiting for us and it is WONDERFUL to see him.

His car is parked nearly outside an airport door, and we soon have our bags and ourselves inside the car. He begins driving us to the main road that will take us to The Hague and his home where we will stay. Yes, what fun it is to be with Marco! We have known him and Irene a long time and every moment with them is fun!

I met them a few years ago when I had a wooden peace pole needing to be taken inside the Congress Hall at The Hague for the 100th anniversary of the first international peace conference held between Queen Wilhelmina of The Netherlands and her cousin Czar Nicholas II of Russia. In the Congress Hall, I placed the peace pole in front of a door with the sign 'Meditation Room', and I soon learned that the woman in charge of the meditation room was Irene. We became immediate friends and she said the peace pole should be planted in front of the Peace Palace. Permission would be needed by the City Fathers and she would ask them. Well, yes, Irene did get permission,

When I first met Irene a few years ago at the 100th anniversary of the first international peace conference, she told me she wanted at her house one evening a 'table conference' of people attending the 100th anniversary. She wanted me to invite those who should come.

Well, I did not know anyone at the conference, but I knew that was not a good enough excuse to give Irene. And so I 'kept my eyes open' for possibilities.

One person, a Japanese male, passed me more than once as I attended the peace conference. The third time he passed me, I stopped him and I told him that Irene wanted a 'table conference' at her house. Would he be interested in attending? Yes!

That is how I first met Hideo Nakazawa of Japan, and we have been friends ever since. In fact, we often SKYPE in order to send peace prayers to Mother Earth as well as to particular areas in trouble in the world.

Well, years ago at The Hague when I first spoke with Hideo Nakazawa and he said 'yes' to attending a 'table conference' at Irene's apartment, I pointed to a man sitting nearby and I said that man looked to be a good person for the table conference. Did Hideo Nakazawa know him?

YES. The two were good friends, and this friend's name was Dr. Masaru Emoto of Japan! He was invited to Irene's table and he was happy to accept.

That evening was SPECIAL.

Several years later, Dr. Emoto, who became a world famous water man, invited Margaret and me to attend a conference around his big table in Tokyo and we attended.

You see how small this world is?

———————

As for this year, 2016, when I arrive at the apartment of Marco and Irene, I meet a third occupant, a big black cat named Mia. I vividly remember her, and as I kneel to pet her, she swishes her tail back and forth as if she remembers me.

Well, there is one thing I remember that I will counter this time. Mia loves to sleep at night on one's head, and she does this by leaping heavily on one's chest before crawling, nails out, onto one's head.

On this visit, no thank you.

For Mia's exit to and from apartment rooms and also to exit to the outside, Marco and Irene have small, round holes in the glass. For the outside exit, a tapestry shields the glass hole from the wind and cold.

———————————

It is time to eat, and we sit around the big table eating and catching up on news and deciding what to do this afternoon. Addressing the water at The Netherlands is our first option, and we pile into the car to head toward a nearby seashore to see the Sand Motor.

What is the Sand Motor?

Here, near the city of The Hague, the Dutch have created in the sea a hook-shaped peninsula of sand to retain the coastline and to make the coastline even bigger. This has been a great endeavor and it has been successful.

I knew that The Netherlanders have always been aware of potential threats from the sea, but I did not realize that about a third of the country is below sea level.

Where Margaret and I landed at Schiphol Airport, this is the world's lowest positioned airport -- thirty-two feet below sea level.

Wow!

The Dutch are continually aware of water and it is continually tested for contamination.

Marco drives Margaret and me to the place where there is the Sand Motor and when we leave the car, the two walk directly to the sandy shoreline for Margaret to draw Vortexes and to ring the Blessings Chimes.*

*See Glossary: Blessings Chimes and David J. Adams.

I stay further back from the shoreline to 'feel' the place, and I notice immediately that it has a calm, cheerful atmosphere. People are peacefully walking near the water and others are seated on the sand further back. Some are picnicking.

Birds, mostly black, are flying overhead or seated briefly on structures. One is walking on the sand near me, and I softly say hello to it. It pauses, listens, and decides to walk nearer to me. I note there is no fear.

I have already surmised that the Dutch are not aggressive toward each other or toward animals and birds. The black bird slowly approaching me knows it will not receive aggression from me.

I need to write more about the Sand Motor. There is water between the shoreline and a long stretch of a sand dune paralleling the water immediately beside it. A man and his dog are walking on this long sand dune, and then I watch as the dog begins running and running and running on the sand dune.

From my view, I note that the sand dune stops and then there is a short stretch of water before the next long stretch of sand dune begins. When the dog reaches this short stretch of water, he does not pause, and in less than a few seconds, he is racing on the next sand dune.

His owner, who does not seem perturbed by the racing actions of the dog, walks rather briskly, and I watch when he reaches the short stretch of water. This does not slow him and I am thinking that this water is very, very shallow.

Is it a moment of low tide?

In any case, it is fun being here at the Sand Motor, seeing the endeavors of the Dutch to bring more land to The Netherlands.

————————

By the end of the day, we are outside the Peace Palace, which is quite close to Irene and Marco's apartment. At the granite peace pole, we encircle it with flowers that have fallen nearby. Now, Marco uses a compass to show North, South, East, West directions. This information will be used during tomorrow's ceremony. He and Irene have been given permission to have a special ceremony near the Peace Palace on September 21.

And yes, September 21, we are here at 8 a.m. to organize this ceremony, which, in many ways, resembles a Native American ceremony.

First, a wide circle is made with a rope on the ground, and this rope is covered by long-stemmed, white flowers. In the center of the circle, at 10 a.m., a fire is built, a sacred fire that will continue until 6 p.m. Coal and other ashes from earlier fires are added.

This sacred fire is for the saying of prayers for peace, healing, good will, etc. Everyone is invited to join in, and regularly more do join in. Irene and Marco are saying that all people are indigenous people. All are one. Everyone is given an opportunity to speak or perform in whatever manner is familiar to them. For over fifteen minutes, a woman sings prayers from India and we are asked to join with her. A Dutch male reads The Fuji Declaration which invites all people and organizations around the world to live in harmony with each other.*

*See Glossary: The Fuji Declaration.

When twelve noon arrives, the Peace Palace begins sounding its gongs, and it continues a long time.

Yes, this is a special day here at The Hague, and I am surprised when a nearby road is blocked because that road will reach the King of The Netherlands who is speaking. Margaret and I are told that to give this speech, the King is taken somewhere in his golden chariot but this time he will not be using his golden chariot. Instead, he will be riding in a glass chariot.

_____

When the September 21 International Day of Peace is finished, Irene and Marco take us to a temple dedicated to Nehalennia, a goddess who was worshipped for both sea and land reasons. Meaning, both sailors and farmers venerated her. For centuries, the Dutch have had a tradition of venerating gods and goddesses.*

*See Glossary: Nehalennia, ancient goddess.

I am learning that mythology today in The Netherlands dates from pre-Christian times, the time of the Roman Empire, and the early Middle Ages.

Marco and Irene have a close friend who is an expert on mythology, and we journey in the car to his home where he and two dogs join us to ride along with us as he points out the home bases of this goddess and that goddess.

I prefer to think of the interesting scenery of Holland, the forests and lagoons, rather than all these being under the control of a goddess.

In any case, it is fun riding around in the car looking at the scenery. And, by the way, before I finish this chapter, I want to point out that the car is ten years old and in perfect shape, as if it was born this year. IT IS AN ELECTRIC CAR.

Wow!

One does not have to stop every few minutes to buy gas!

From Margaret:

September 18:

When it is time to leave for The Netherlands, Joan, the taxi driver, comes to pick us up and we give her our latest book. She says she will read it while waiting at the airport for her customers to arrive.

We have a fast flight to Newark, New Jersey. On the way, we see the New York City skyline -- the Empire State Building, Freedom Tower, the Statue of Liberty.

At Newark Airport, we wait a long time for our next plane which leaves at 6:00 p.m. While waiting, we talk to a Swedish lady whose husband is English, and they live in Rotterdam, The Netherlands. She has been waiting a long time at this airport and so we give her one of our books to read. She is happy and says she will begin reading it immediately.

She tells us that the people in Rotterdam have to drain the foundations of their houses every 50-60 years. This is done mostly by hand and they have to drain and refill the foundations.

When Barbara and I board our plane to Amsterdam, I watch movies and sleep. The flight is smooth.

———————————

September 19:

We arrive at 7:10 a.m. and Marco Hadjidakis is here to pick us up to drive us to his and Irene's home in The Hague. On arrival, we sit in their garden to talk, have tea and cookies, and then take a nap.

At 5:30 p.m., we are ready to go to the Dunes of The Hague to see the new manmade sand spit curving outwards. This shifts sand to expand the shoreline and protect the land. It is an experiment called Sand Motor.

While Irene goes shopping, Marco, Barbara and I examine the Sand Motor project. A large lagoon has been formed behind the sand bar at the ocean called the North Sea. Barbara sits to overview everything while Marco and I walk to a point on the lagoon where the high tide comes in.

Here, Marco plays the Tibetan brass chimes and I ring the Blessings Chimes for the waters and life in the waters. The two chimes harmonize with each other and the water. Marco sings and I watch the wave currents and wind currents flowing with the singing.

Now I draw the Vortex Symbols at the lagoon shoreline, and the energy is strong of the Vortex of Light, Sound, and Vibration. Also very strong are the Symbols for Universal Law of Perception and the Spiritual Law of Future Sight.

After putting down the Vortexes, the sun makes great shafts of Light. Then three shafts become one. I feel this glory sky acknowledging the Vortexes and sending the power outwards.

Sea gulls call out.

POWER. Love and Healing.

Marco and I bless the ocean and I make a small sacred design of shells placed in the four directions. Then we turn and face the land and we read together the Vortexes for the whole continent of Europe. When we finish, we walk to meet Barbara who is surrounded by birds.

Afterward, we meet Irene for dinner at an Italian restaurant where we have delicious local fish.

We watch the powerful sunset.

It has been a beautiful day on our first day in Holland.

Tomorrow we will use the Vortex of Right Relationship and the Vortex of Growth to set the ceremony for the International Day of Peace at the Peace Palace.

————————

September 20:

The morning is quiet and cool. We drive to the Peace Palace where nearby we will have a celebration tomorrow. We stop at a granite peace pole and we place red geranium blossoms around it.

————————

September 21:

At 7:00 a.m., we have packed the car and a small carriage hitched to it that is filled with brooms, drums, horn, and wood for the fire, etc. It does not take us long to drive to the Peace Palace to set up across the street what is required for a Rainbow Circle and a sacred fire. It is my understanding that the meaning of the Rainbow Circle is a circle for people representing our world of different races, creeds and colors. All are welcome here. The sacred fire gives focus to a world peace event being held here at the Peace Palace. It will burn between 10:00 a.m. and 6:00 p.m.

Marco and Irene's friends come early to help sweep the area, hang the peace banners, and prepare for the lighting of the sacred fire. For the Rainbow Circle, a heavy braided rope is laid down in a circle and I help place clusters of white flowers on top of the rope – long-stemmed daisies, roses and mums.

A woman passes walking her dog, a Welch Terrier, and the dog immediately stops and wants to join in the celebration for peace. The woman is hurrying to keep an appointment but the dog refuses to budge. He flattens himself on the ground and will not move an inch. He totally wants to be here knowing this is an important place to be. I think he wants to represent animals. Well, the woman owner pulls him away, but another small dog comes and takes his place.

The animals are represented!

At 10:00 a.m. the sacred fire is lit. Now each person comes individually close to the fire to be smudged and to speak a prayer. At the fire, I speak about my quandary. How can I carry this beautiful fire to all the oceans and seas? I receive channeling which I speak aloud:

Margaret you can take the Spirit of the Fire to the ocean. It is powerful and the energy can be spread around the entire world – for the sea life — for the whales, dolphins, fish, etc.

People are gathering and gathering and they come forward to speak. At noontime, there is a Minute of Silence for peace and for the cessation of war. I know that this moment is being performed around the world at noon in each time zone.

After the noon meditation, The Fuji Declaration is read by Mr. Leo van der Vlist, director of the Netherlands Centre For Indigenous Peoples. The declaration speaks of the unification of humanity through understanding that everyone on the planet has a Divine Spark that seeks a life of unity, compassion and love, wisdom and joy. Peace will come when the basic oneness of humanity is understood and honored while celebrating diversity and embracing unity.

I think to myself that one day this International Day of Peace will become everyday.

May Peace Prevail On Earth.

The ceremony continues with singing, chanting, and drumming. At one point, Barbara and I walk a short way to Café Blossom for a brief lunch. Here we meet two delightful Dutch women who have also been attending the ceremony and we eat with them.

When we return to the ceremony in front of the Peace Palace, we first visit the World Flame and the Peace Tree near the entrance to the Peace Palace. Then we return to singing at the sacred fire and I ring the Blessing Chimes.

Today has a supreme feeling of peace and goodwill shared by all. Someone remarks that we are not writing history, we are creating the future.

Tonight we are rewarded with a beautiful sunset of gold, pink, and blue.

————————

September 22:

4:00 a.m., I am up early thinking about yesterday's International Day of Peace ceremony. Emma comments:*

*See Glossary: Emma Kuntz.

Yesterday, the music, singing, drumming, prayers and the fire linked the dimensions and called in the ancestors of the land. Many beings were there yesterday – the Angelic Beings, Brothers and Sisters from Higher Worlds, and the Golden Dolphins.

Reciprocity -- the circling around about water. The Holland dike system – the making of new land from water and the giving back land to the sea.

Holland is the land of the sea. That is why the people are so attuned to dolphins and whales. Here is where the whales and dolphins once came to give birth and later to die.

There are many traditions floating around in Holland. The Dutch are open-hearted – the spiritual Dutch. They are seafarers and voyagers. Still today seeking paths/approaches through the ceremonies of other lands. They are now discovering the traditions, ceremonies of this land.

The Dutch are full out passionate in their projects. The key is to find the right projects to apply this pressure of will and enthusiasm. It is fitting that the Peace Palace is built here and influences here and all peoples who come to The Hague. It is the United Nations on the streets and in the neighborhood blocks.

Margaret, you look for the lace curtains of years ago. No longer are they here. The sun and time have taken them away. Now the windows are open to the straight direct light of the sun. The Dutch have always loved light and delicate pattern. Look at the exquisite floral scarves and embroidered coats – the flowers speak in the paintings, embroideries, rugs, tiles. The sacred fire circle was ringed with white flowers. The symbol of the Rainbow Circle gathering was the double rainbow -- a circle top and bottom -- reflecting the Universal Law of Symmetry. The trees reflect the Spiritual Law of Equality.
Holland is based on strong individuality -- each person a gift. Openness, truth speaking, and compassionate.

———————

In the morning, we drive to Colijnsplaat to visit the Temple to Nehalennia, Goddess of the waters and bounty of the land. Also, she protects the sea people, the land people, and young ones.

The temple is two-storey with six columns on the front and seven on the sides. Inside there is an altar with an ancient sculpture of Nehalennia seated with fruit in a basket and an alert dog at her side.

To the left we see a modern sculpture of Nehalennia, full height, abstract, with a boat and dog at her side. She is holding a basket of fruit and her hands resemble fish tails.

Barbara feels the essence of Mary, Mother of the Christ. I feel the sea, the pull of the sea coming to the land and the land people going out to sea. The sea and the land are one.

Nehalennia bridges the past and the future through the dimensions, opening to other times and space.

To her, Irene and Marco drum and sing the Divine Star Woman of the Sea and another song of peace. Our hearts are lifted.

Then we leave and take a long ride north to De Koningsherberg Inn at Anloo where we stay the night and have a delicious dinner.

———————

September 23:

Early in the morning, I channel Nehalennia, and I ask her to speak to me.

She answers: Take the light beam from the Sun and let it dance on each element -- the grass, the trees, the water, the land. It is love that grows the fruit, the apple -- the gift of the trees, the gift of the rain, the gift of the sunlight – all contained in the perfection of the apple.

The apple is created by the Spirits of Nature, given each year as the earth progresses across space dancing and spinning around the Great Sun.

Loosen the mind. Relax the will. Let the heart sense the growing power of Nature -- the richness of the soil, the strength of the water -- in the oceans, in the tides -- the coming and the going of fluidity – the moving of the clouds – the crisp air – gifts of life to the people and all life forms on the planet.

Walk in gratitude for this special entity, Mother Earth, who gives and provides all this bounty. Gratitude to the trees. Gratitude to the rocks and soil that are the groundwork of life on this planet at this time.

Release the mind. Open the heart. Smile at the trees and at each other. Make the stranger a friend. You are the same, in different presentation – the heart is the same – the container of the heart, the body and its decoration different -- the mind different and yet the same on the emotional level. The mind directs. Let it be wise and balanced.

Move off the center point of the self and expand outwards to the universe. There are universes in all life systems. Relax the mind and join the whole infinity of creation. The boat of love assures smooth sailing. The sailor knows the elements and the tides. Open your senses to what is around you. Go forward and embrace the day. Thinking too much wears down the mind. Let spontaneity come forth. Let the intuition and heart guide the way.

Blessings and Love,
Nehalennia

_____

8:00 a.m., we begin driving to pick up a friend who knows the history of this area, and as we move along, I note there are different levels of energy -- some good, some bad. When they are not so good, I ask that we stop for me to ring the Blessings Chimes for the trees, land, agriculture, houses and ancient past. Then I draw and speak the Vortexes.

In the late afternoon, we are at Lelystad, a city built on reclaimed land from the sea, founded in 1967 and named after the engineer who made the reclamation possible. The city is 3 meters (9.8 feet) below sea level. I see ancient tall ships in the harbor LOCATED ABOVE the farmland and houses. Literally, physically above! There is a large new marina with many boats of all sizes and new apartment buildings and restaurants close by.

The whole area is called Flevoland, the twelfth province of Holland, established in 1986 where islands were connected by dikes. This is reclaimed land from what was the Zuiderzee. Now many people live here.

What a joy to see this. What a grand accomplishment. The dike stands between the new land and the water.

_____

September 24:

Last night we have returned to The Hague, and now I am up at 8:00 a.m. slowly packing. As I pack, I review in my mind the beautiful thatched roofs of straw that we saw near Anloo. Barns and houses stand as one unit with roofs extended down to the top of the first floor. The family quarters have bright windows on the side facing the road. Flowers decorate the entrance and window boxes.

I also relish the thought of seeing the tall masts of sailing ships high above the land in Conlijnsplaat and Lelystad where many people live on land below sea level.

At noon, Irene drives Barbara and me to the Peace Palace before we return to our home in America. Now we have a surprise. The Peace Palace has become a center for a huge Peace Run! Thousands of runners! We park the car and cheer the runners.

I clap and give encouragement for their efforts. Irene films the race. When the runners have passed us, I ring the Blessings Chimes. Then we go to the entrance gate area of the Peace Palace and write our prayers for peace to hang on the Peace Tree there where many have already put their prayers.

When leaving, I look up and see a dolphin cloud and a star cloud above the Peace Palace. A blessing for this amazing trip.

==

CHAPTER 4

Philadelphia

Joint Journals:

First from Barbara:

October 2016, an election for the next President is coming to this country, the U.S.A. I need to understand better how leaders of our country were selected years ago when our country became independent. What is the background?

We need to go to Philadelphia, which, I understand, is the home for the 'beginnings' of choosing who would run the country.

When Philadelphia was growing into an important place in 1774, it was the site of the First Continental Congress, a meeting where the American colonies met to draw up a message to King George III of Great Britain concerning the Rights of those living on the new land.

Because the message was not followed, in 1775 the colonies met again and called themselves the Second Continental Congress. This, too, was not followed. In 1776, when representatives of the colonies met another time, they agreed to unite by calling themselves Free and Independence States, the United States of America. On July 4, 1776, a Declaration of Independence was adopted, and this adoption was held in Independence Hall, Philadelphia.

This year, 2016, the U.S.A. will have an important election on November 8, and so, I think it is important that we know the background of how Presidents are elected.

———————

October 23:

This morning we are on the phone checking flights to Philadelphia. Taking the train would be too slow. This would mean eight hours to New York City and then waiting to change trains to Philadelphia. Once that is done, there are a few more hours on a train to reach our destination.

We phone American Airlines and that is a godsend! Margaret has enough accumulated mileage to have a free round-trip ticket. I can have a free one-way trip and my credit card will pay for the remainder. We can take a 5:30 morning flight directly to Philadelphia. There is no need to stop in New York City or elsewhere to catch a flight to Philadelphia!

As for finding a hotel to stay overnight on Monday, Hotels.com finds us a room. If the cost is divided in half between Margaret and me, we pay forty dollars each! And there is another advantage. Every half hour there is a free hotel shuttle going to and from the airport!

And so, the next day, Monday morning, 4:15 a.m., our dependable taxi service picks us up and drives us to the airport where, because we have our tickets via the Internet, we go directly through Security (without a hitch) and we wait at the gate for our flight to leave.

Well, here is our first and only hitch. The desk attendant at our departure gate tells us there will be a half-hour delay and we will leave at 6 a.m. rather than 5:30 a.m. Yet, she tells us, we will probably arrive at 7 a.m., our expected arrival time. We are in no rush to arrive at such an early hour.

Why does the plane leave late? The desk attendant tells us the plane has arrived late last night, and there is a rule that the flight crew must have a certain time period on the ground before handling the next flight. We must wait. Well, again, we are not in a rush and we sit and wait patiently with the other passengers.

And yes, the plane, which is a Canadian plane operated by American Airlines, is full. Thirteen rows of two seats each on both sides of the aisle with the exception of the last row that has only two seats. One side of the aisle has the toilet.

I am seated on row 12 and no one is seated in the two seats behind me. I do not understand why these seats are empty, but maybe there is a need to have a seat or two available in case another flight is overbooked or canceled or whatever. This plane can help handle the matter.

In any case, once we are off the ground, I note that the flight is comfortable and fast. This small plane does not jump around but seems determined to arrive as soon as possible.

On arrival at Philadelphia, it is still dark, but there is plenty of activity at the airport by employees darting here and there with their carts. This is a HUGE airport! And yes, when we deplane and walk up the enclosed ramp to reach the interior of a terminal, I am surprised at the number of people scurrying here and there to reach their flights. It is, after all, only 7 a.m.

Now it is time to figure out the location of the hotel phone panel so we can phone our hotel to ask for a free shuttle. Yes, this is a big terminal, but a number of employees are working, and so we have no difficulty receiving a positive answer to our question. We are to go here and there and downstairs and around this corner, etc.

It takes time, but we do find the hotel phone panel, and the hotel called Microtel Inn & Suites tells us there will be a free shuttle, a blue van, at the airport within minutes. We must wait for it at the proper place. And yes, when it arrives, we see the name of the hotel brightly painted on the blue van's exterior.

The driver is friendly and fun to talk with. He asks us why we have come to Philadelphia, and when we tell him we want to investigate how our country was founded, he immediately suggests that we should sign up with a bus tour company that will take us to the important places in the city, such as Congress Hall, the Independence Hall, the Liberty Bell Center, the National Constitution Center, etc.

This sounds exactly what we need to do and he will phone the bus company to put us on the list for a 9 a.m. pick up at the bus starting point. He says the bus will make stops 27 times for us to get off and then on again whenever we want.

At the hotel, we identify ourselves at the front desk and talk with the manager who is from India. He says we can have breakfast if we want. It is free and the tables and chairs and food are just there ahead of him. Rather than eating, we sit near the front desk with two women from Thailand waiting for a taxi to the airport to catch their early flight. They do not know about the hotel's free shuttle service.

I have had interesting experiences in Thailand and so we sit and talk.

Then the desk manager says our hotel room is cleaned and ready for us, which is a surprise! It is so early, we intended to leave our bags with him at the front desk while we are away. But no, we can leave our bags in our room. He personally takes us to the room, and it is close to the front desk. When we open the door, it seems as if this is a new room that no one has yet occupied.

Everything about this Philadelphia trip is unfolding BEAUTIFULLY!!!

Just before 9 a.m., the hotel gives us a free shuttle to the starting point of the tour buses that announce on their sides in bold letters, Big B Bus Tour of Philadelphia. Hop On Hop Off. Several big buses are parked here, and I realize that all these buses will be stopping at the same 27 places. Our ticket means we can get on or off any of these buses.

And now comes another wonderful surprise. Less than a three-minute walk from the bus starting point is exactly what is of great importance for Margaret and me -- The Independence Visitor Center! Here is where one can receive a free ticket to enter Independence

Hall, the location where the present-day government of the U.S.A. was founded.

Of course, entering this place is of great interest for most coming to Philadelphia to learn about the past, and so tickets are often in short supply. Margaret and I race across the street and then we race on bright colored red brick to reach the Independence Visitor Center. We enter it just as the Independence Hall ticket booth opens, and we stand in line waiting for those in front of us to receive their tickets.

When it is our turn, we learn that the first available tickets start at 2 p.m., and we take two of them. We are told that we must be there at the entrance at 1:50 p.m., and I assume that if we are late, others will take our place. In other words, don't be late!

This Visitor Center is LARGE and we are in no rush to leave it. Videos of Colonial times are playing and we watch two of them. One describes Philadelphia at the time of the Revolution and the writing of the Declaration of Independence and the drafting and ratification of the Constitution.

The other film shows the life of young people affected by the events of the Colonial period -- the transition between being a colony and being a nation.

There is so much to see at the Visitor Center! And, there is an inviting display of food that can be eaten here. We are hungry and we eat.

Now we need to pay attention to our watches that are telling us we should be thinking about our tickets that will allow us to enter nearby Independence Hall at 2 p.m. We leave the Visitor Center and walk a short way to the Liberty Bell Center. This is a spectacular building. And then we walk behind the Liberty Bell Center to Independence Hall. To our knowledge, we think we are too early to enter Independence Hall, but now we encounter a park ranger who tells us we can enter early if we first go through Security.

Security? We did not know Security would be involved with us visiting Independence Hall.

Well, we have nothing to worry about, and so, of course, we should go through Security so we can enter Independence Hall early.

And yes, Security was quick and easy.

Now, just as we finish Security, a line of people standing at the door begins to move into the building. We quickly line up with them and enter a room with a large circle of chairs. Already most chairs are taken by the newly-entered people, but there are two chairs available and Margaret and I take them.

What is happening? Why have the people been allowed to enter?

I think I've figured this out. When the building is empty because earlier tours have left, then the building is opened for those waiting. The time of 2 p.m. does not need to be observed by us.

The park ranger in charge of the newly-formed group is quite young, tall, nearly seven feet tall, with an African American background and he has a strong, well-seasoned voice for speaking with those who have come to learn about Independence Hall and about the forming of the government of the United States of America.

Well, our quick journey to Philadelphia moves from beginning to end with pleasant surprises throughout.

Now it is time for Margaret to write you about Philadelphia.

From Margaret:

Before Barbara and I go to Philadelphia, my mind is spinning. There is so much for me to review and to learn. I ask Emma and the Christ to clarify what I need to know.

Response: Go back to Philadelphia, the City of Brotherly Love, the source of the founding principles of the country. It is a city of peace, equality of being, unity of purpose and of life. Equalitarianism, openness, truth, justice.

The city holds the key. It is in the keystone state, Pennsylvania, center of the thirteen original colonies. It is the foundation stone of the Declaration of Independence and of the Constitution.

William Penn, founder of the state, was open to the high principles of freedom and equality. Gather up the energy field of the original high principles. Let the concept of the City of Brotherly Love hold up the flames of peace, liberty, equality, freedom, justice and truth.

Write the concepts. Theses are the standards, the ideals to uphold when reviewing today's discourse.

I am grateful for the comments of Emma and the Christ and later I ask for more comments. I receive from them:

You are seeking unity of purpose, the greatest good for the people. You have seen the condition of the water environment, the land and air environment. Much decision-making has been made with short-time thoughts, with little consideration for the long-term impact on the land, on the people, on the planet.

Look at the gifts given from the gathering at Philadelphia – the unity of the states, the uniting of the people under one government that protects the rights of Life, Liberty, and the pursuit of Happiness.

Look at the higher framework and do not get stuck in the particular details. Treat others as you would have them treat you. Honor the Light of each Soul. Address the heart of each person. Acknowledge each person — from the individual, to the family, to the community, to the city, to the state, to the country, to the world.

See the unifying principles which 'ring true' through the centuries to the now, to the beyond. The principles of the Vortexes give clarity to this understanding – the balancing of systems. Play with this. Do not get heavy. You have to carry this understanding in your heart. The mind likes complexities. The heart loves the Truth.

I know there is also a need to include in my thoughts William Penn who founded Pennsylvania as a society of equality and freedom of religion. Also, the Declaration of Independence proclaiming the inalienable Right to Life, Liberty and the Pursuit of Happiness. And I am thinking of ancient Philadelphia in Asia Minor, which was an early church reflecting the strength and teachings of Christ.

There is so much to think about. Again, I ask Emma and the Christ to comment.

Answer: They are high principles of understandings. Times in history when things were changing. There was a bedrock of Love and compassion in action in ancient Asia Minor, and there was a bedrock of Love and compassion in Philadelphia during the foundation of the new country. All are based on love, unity and equality, witnessing the Light of each person.

Shafts of Light over time. Use this Light to read the present dialogue. Let this Light give clarity to the country in the present. Let your heart be lifted up. There is a strong foundation here. Uncover it and let it shine. Let the people honor the base of those who have gone before and lighted the way. Love is the highest principle. It endures over time and does not cease, but ever expands.

———————

October 24:

Barbara has already written about our journey to Philadelphia, the hotel, Big B Bus Tour, and Independence Hall, but I want to write more here at our stop at the Visitor Center. We see two excellent films.

The first film, *Independence*, tells the story of the founding of the United States from the viewpoint of Benjamin Franklin, John Adams and others. We witness the debates and see the factors that led to the decision to break from England and to form a new country of United States. The film brings alive the complexity and effort of the writing and the signing of the Declaration of Independence in 1776 and the Constitution in 1787.

The second film, *Choosing Sides,* tells the story of four young people and how they reacted to the changing times as the country went from individual colonies to a new nation. There were views of a young woman pacifist, a soldier wanting to fight, a political young man, and a married woman loyal to England. Their thoughts and dreams were captured in their diaries which gave insight into what was happening in 1776 Philadelphia. The film was a fantastic way of presenting history.

Later, when we visit Independence Hall, we go to the Courtroom of the Pennsylvania Supreme Court that once displayed the British king's coat of arms. Then it was replaced with the coat of arms of the Commonwealth of Pennsylvania.

In the Assembly Room where The Declaration of Independence and U.S. Constitution were signed, tables and chairs are arranged as if the signers had just left the room. This room holds inviting memories of dreams and promises to be fulfilled by the future generations. I thank those who had gathered here. Barbara and I are here today to honor their foresight.

It is wonderful experiencing the past. I think Philadelphia should be visited from time to time so memories of setting up governing for the country can remembered.

When it is time to return to the hotel, Barbara and I ride in a shuttle with a driver who begins taking us to the hotel. He is a replacement driver and becomes lost. Suddenly we are on Governor Printz Boulevard. I used to live in the Philadelphia area and I remember this boulevard. I ask myself, is this the old King's Highway that linked the original colonies? It may be part of the route that linked Philadelphia, Maryland and Virginia, and in fact, Boston in Massachusetts to Charleston, South Carolina. I am thinking of the distances traveled *to form a more perfect union*, a statement in the Preamble of the United States Constitution.

==================================

CHAPTER 5

Farmington Quaker Meeting

J oint Journals:

From Barbara:

Margaret and I receive a notice of an October 22-23 event called the 200th Anniversary Celebration at the 1816 Farmington Quaker Meetinghouse, New York State, about an hour's drive for us.

Why should this event be of interest to us? We are not Quakers, but we respect what the Farmington Quakers did for this country. As an example, the homeland of the Native American Senecas was in this area and became threatened by being uprooted and forced to live much further west. The Senecas did not want to move, and they appealed to the Farmington Quakers to help prevent this uprooting. And yes, the Farmington Quakers immediately and strongly responded to this appeal. Many, many letters were written to government officials, petitions were sent out, and speakers voiced their support for allowing the Senecas to remain in their homeland.

The Seneca appeal to remain was granted, and today the Senecas still live in their homeland.

At the time of 1816. the Farmington Quakers also supported the rights of women, such as the right to vote, and this right of women to vote eventually became successful.

A third important movement, supporting proper treatment of former African slaves, was successfully supported by the Quakers.

Today, 2016, the 1816 Farmington Quaker Meetinghouse is ready to be celebrated for its efforts, and Margaret and I wish to join this celebration, which is open to all.

A couple days before the celebration, we drive there and we discover that reaching Farmington by car is not easy. A major road has been closed and we find ourselves lost.

Well, we want none of THAT. Before it is time to go to the Farmington celebration, we approach AAA, a travel agency, to ask for driving directions that will not make us lost.

And yes, the AAA directions are EXCELLENT and we have no problem reaching the 1816 Farmington Quaker Meetinghouse on October 22. In fact, we arrive early.

But, the weather is a bit uncooperative. The wind is blowing HARD and the temperature is hovering around COLD. We are wearing four layers of clothes that can be reduced to two when we reach the Meetinghouse. Well, when we arrive, we realize the celebration will not be in the Meetinghouse itself, but in a large, white tent erected nearby. The wind LOVES the tent. It blows hard and the tent flaps its sides so the sides lift and the cold roars in.

What is inside? About fifty chairs for the celebration audience. Because we are early, few are in the tent and so we have our choice of seats. Well, there is only one proper choice -- chairs next to a big, portable heater blasting hot air onto a couple chairs close to the heater. Also, we have two blankets in the car, and these two blankets are soon wrapped around us.

At 11 a.m. sharp, the celebration begins with a welcome to everyone by two members of the Meetinghouse board. Then a traditional Seneca thanksgiving is given by Seneca Peter Jemison, director of the Ganondagan State Historic Site, which has a new center called the Seneca Art & Culture Center.

Margaret and I were there a couple years ago when Jemison opened this new center, and today we appreciate that he is speaking in the same manner here in Farmington. First, he introduces himself in the Seneca language and then he explains in English that he will be giving us a full greeting in Seneca followed by a translation in English.

I enjoyed his earlier greeting at the new Ganondagan center and I want to tell you a small incident that happened there when he was telling us that water for drinking was brought there. Just where Margaret and I were standing outside the new center listening to him, waist-high water fountains beside us began pouring out water. What a shock!

Well, there are no water foundations inside the tent at Farmington, but we did receive a tiny cup holding corn laced with maple syrup. It was DELICIOUS!

After Peter Jemison, others of importance speak a few words, including some portraying themselves as historic figures wearing traditional historic clothes.

I recognize the names of Frederick Douglass, Susan B. Anthony and Elizabeth Cady Stanton.

Yes, I enjoyed attending this celebration.

Now, Margaret will give her memories of Farmington.

From Margaret,

October 22:

We begin our journey to Farmington by using a trip planner from AAA, a travel agency. It is a cold and rainy morning and we are wearing our winter jackets, scarves, glove, etc.

When we arrive at Farmington at 10:15 a.m., we see an old meetinghouse that is to be restored and a big tent in front of it. The program for the day will be in the tent.

Helpful men are ready to guide us to park the car, and then we walk to the tent. The wind is blowing and there is a chill to the air. No longer do we have the warm sun and balmy weather of a week ago. Mother Earth is blessing the land with rain.

Inside the tent, we sign in and we are greeted by friendly women who say they are happy we are here. We walk to front seats to sit close to the speaker's table, but then we spot a portable heater blowing warm air three rows back. We change our location to join a friendly man already settled in front of the heater.

There is time before the ceremony begins and after I have a chair, I slip outside to enter the old meetinghouse that is just outside the tent. I have learned that this old building used to be in a different location but it has been moved and it will be restored.

The old meetinghouse building stands directly on the ground. Its floor is dirt and the rafters are split logs. The wooden framework holds the memories of those who spoke and prayed here. Memories started flooding back and tears came to my eyes. Somehow I have been drawn to this powerful place. I am alone and the building speaks to me to continue what has started here -- important history.

Why did we come to Farmington today? It is the 1816 anniversary of the founding of the Farmington Quaker Meetinghouse. Focus here has been on high ideals -- the rights of the native people to keep their land, the rights of the African Americans to have their dignity as free citizens of the country, and the right of half the population, the women, to vote.

A great number of Farmington Quakers participated in the women's vote movement which began in 1848. It took until 1919 for Congress to pass the 19th Amendment granting women the right to vote and until 1920 for it to be ratified. Now we are having a woman candidate in the election of 2016 and we have the possibility of a first woman President. It has taken a long time to witness this.

———————

Inside today's tent celebration, volunteers are at tables and one group is compiling a list of the descendants of the original families of the 1816 Quaker Meetinghouse. We are asked, are we possible descendants? No, but we wish the volunteers well. I feel they will find many descendants coming here today.

Across the way is a table with volunteers from the Seneca community handing out samples of hot corn mush with maple syrup. This is made of Iroquois white corn that has been preserved in its original form. It is delicious, hot, and wards off the chill.

The 200th Anniversary Celebration program begins with the telling of the history of the 1816 Quaker Meetinghouse and the long tradition of a close association with the local Native American people, the Senecas. It was that close association that made the Seneca women tell the Quaker women that they were being forced to move and they did not want to leave their land.

The Quakers immediately began setting up a letter-writing campaign, sending out pamphlets, and also connecting to the Philadelphia Quakers. Great efforts resulted in the local native people staying where they were and not moving across the Mississippi.

After an official welcome by Farmington Meeting board member, Peter Jemison gives a traditional Seneca Thanksgiving Address both in Seneca and in English. He speaks of the people coming together and their minds becoming one.

When Ronnie Reitter of the Seneca Nation speaks, she tells us of the Peacemaker who came 1200 years ago bringing the Great Law of Peace that later influenced the U.S. Constitution. To this she adds, the Native American clan mothers have the responsibility to put a chief into a leadership position. A chief must live up to the role and not overstep. Otherwise, the clan mothers can remove him. She says, men and women walk in balance, shoulder to shoulder.

The next part of the program in the tent is honoring the movement advocating women's right to vote. Early Quakers believed in the equality of all people and so they actively supported this movement.

I love listening to a woman dressed as Elizabeth Cady Stanton, early leader of the women's movement who often spoke at Farmington. Other historic figures are portrayed -- Frederick Douglass, Susan B. Anthony and Lucretia Coffin Mott.

I would like to tell you a bit more about the Quakers, who, as members of The Religious Society of Friends, began in the mid 17th century in England.

They believed in gender, racial and religious freedom for all, and they acted upon the word of God in these important social issues. But, they were persecuted and many left for America. William Penn, a Quaker, founded in 1681 Pennsylvania as a society of equality with freedom of religion. Quakers spread to New England, New York, New Jersey west to Ohio, Indiana and south to Delaware, Maryland, Virginia, the Carolinas and Georgia.

And so, this is the background of the 1816 Farmington Quaker Meetinghouse where everyone has gathered today to celebrate.

==

CHAPTER 6

Niagara Falls

Joint Journals:

From Barbara:

September 1, Margaret and I know we must go to Niagara Falls to connect with the dragon living there who is the spiritual guardian of the North American continent. The continent is in a precarious state and we must go to the dragon to ask for help in soothing the continent.

We phone Hotels.com asking for accommodations at the Sheraton at the Falls Hotel, and we not only receive accommodations, but a big discount because of accumulated credits with Hotels.com. WONDERFUL!

We will stay only one night. That's enough. After speaking today between 2:30 and 3 p.m. on television with Carmen's PAX TV network, we will jump into the car and drive to Niagara Falls. It should take a little more than two hours.

There will be no need to take anything except a raincoat in case it rains, something to wear overnight, and a sweater in case it is cold.

Cold? What is that? The temperature has spent most of the summer at 90 to 100 degrees Fahrenheit.

Rain? We have had little of that. In fact, we have not had enough to satisfy most crops growing in this area. Interesting, Buffalo is to the west of us and we have heard there was much rain this summer. How far is Buffalo from Niagara Falls? Only a stone's throw.

In any case, we will not need to take much to Niagara Falls because we are only staying overnight. While we are there, only one event interests us -- taking the Maid of the Mist boat because it passes the home of the dragon.

Yes, we need to go to Niagara Falls to ask the dragon to help temper the risky condition of the North American continent. Persistent earthquakes are making us nervous. Also, there are too many dormant volcanoes that are beginning to snarl for one reason or another.

And so, just after 3 p.m. today we have thrown a few things into the car and we are on our way to Niagara Falls! Margaret is driving and I am sitting beside her with maps in my hands.

A couple blocks away is the Expressway which will take us to New York State's big Thruway, Route 90. We are soon whizzing along with a generous number of cars, plus BIG trucks that seem to become bigger as the days go by. A few truckers are even driving TWO huge trucks hitched to each other. If needed, can they make a quick stop?

Oh dear!

In any case, we move along smartly and we reach and pass a sign telling us we are in the vicinity of Churchville. Then we pass a sign for Bergen. I am telling Margaret we will soon be seeing a sign for LeRoy, which, I have been told, is the place where jello was first made.

Well, we don't turn off to go to LeRoy, but we know that within a very short time we will be entering the Thruway and receiving a ticket for driving on it. We will be paying $2.00, which we consider generous because we will be driving quite a while on this road.

On the Thruway, we go along to Clarence, a rest area just before we reach the turnoff for Niagara Falls. Here, we stop to ask for a map of Niagara Falls. We have two maps with us but they are not detailed enough to prevent us from getting lost. We feel that other travelers stop at Clarence to ask about reaching specific Niagara Falls destinations.

When we stop, the Clarence Information woman we speak to is pleasant and she gives us two different Niagara Falls maps. With a bright green pen, she automatically begins drawing where we should drive. I think all day she has to draw on maps. I think she can draw in her sleep.

In any case, Margaret and I are soon on our way, and we are quickly at the Thruway exit giving $2.00 to the hand that automatically comes out of a small booth.

And now we are surprised. When we turn off, we begin seeing a number of stopped cars on the other side of the road. A half-mile of stopped cars?

Why?

They are backed up because they have to stop to receive tickets to enter the New York State Thruway!

We make a quick decision. When we leave Niagara Falls, we will not wait in line to get a ticket for the Thruway. We will find another way to return home.

Fortunately, the traffic is not heavy on our side of the road going into Niagara Falls. We move along normally and when we begin reaching the outskirts of the city, the Clarence Information woman's bright green drawing becomes a bit confusing. We go along with uncertainty until we reach a building saying Tourist Information.

Well, that's perfect for us. We stop and a pleasant man tells us to continue straight and we will see two sets of stoplights. Ignore the first set, but at the second set, turn left and we will be on Main Street. Follow that and we will very soon reach 3rd Street, location of our hotel.

And yes, we find our hotel, the Sheraton! It has a big sign on it so one can hardly pass it will out reading the sign. We turn in and park at the door and I run in to show the email I received from Hotels.com.

All is well.

Within a half hour we are eating at a large restaurant on the first floor. We are hungry! When was the last time we ate?

————————

September 2:

Now begins the reason why we have come to Niagara Falls -- to connect with the dragon, spiritual guardian of the North American continent.

But first we eat a peanut butter and honey sandwich made yesterday; we drink water, and we are outside the Sheraton at 7:45 a.m. to take a taxi to the ticket booth for the Maid of the Mist boat ride.

We want the first ride of the day, 9 a.m., and we know the ticket booth is open at 8:30 a.m. This is the beginning of the Labor Day holiday. Probably many have come to Niagara Falls and many will want to ride the Maid of the Mist.

Will they want to eat breakfast before taking the boat?

Yes, I think they will want to eat breakfast and so they cannot take the 9 a.m. boat. But, we have already eaten our breakfast, and so we are very ready to take the 9 a.m. boat!

Parked outside our hotel are tour buses and only one taxi, and the driver is just now exiting the hotel. We ask if we can ride with him and he says he already has customers but he will phone for a taxi for us.

He phones, and yes, soon another taxi arrives and we are in it! He drives along and then stops as close as he can to the ticket booth. We leave his taxi exactly where the last time we took the Maid of the Mist a horse was hitched to a carriage waiting for customers.

We could not be his customer, but we petted his face and he was happy. We had felt sorry for him because he was an old horse looking tired and worn out from driving tourists all day along city streets.

In any case, today there is no horse, and Margaret and I make our way a few hundred feet to the ticket booth area which had no one except a man watering flowers. It is just before 8 a.m. and we know we will be the first to be in line when the booths open at 8:30. Our hopes soar for taking the 9 a.m. boat!

We sit on a bench waiting, watching the flowers being watered. Then an older man with a cane begins slowly walking by our bench and we exchange 'hellos'. Also, we ask if he will be taking the boat. He pauses and says no. He is enjoying himself walking to see the Falls.

And then, a wonderful conversation begins between us. The man tells us he has been around the world five times and yet he has never visited Niagara Falls. He is on his way to New York City to visit his son, and he has decided he will first visit Niagara Falls.

He is wearing a shirt with Wi lettering on it and we ask if he is from Wisconsin. No. He has been all his life as a tugboat man who fixes tugboats. Now he is involved with a museum that wants tugboats on display and he is requested to see whether or not all the mechanical features are operating correctly.

Who has ever met a tugboat person? Certainly, Margaret and I have not, and we are interested. He tells us there were tugboats used during the invasion of Normandy in World War II and there were tugboats during the Vietnam War.

Wow! Whoever heard of that!

This man is so much fun to listen to that we forget to watch for the opening of the ticket booths for the Maid of the Mist! People have begun to line up to buy tickets.

We say good-bye to the tugboat man and hurry to the ticket booths to buy tickets. Our money is taken immediately and so we realize there is room on the 9 a.m. boat. Good!

Now we meet a friend and her two children living on the Canadian side of Niagara Falls, and they have come across the border to see us. We make plans to see them again after Margaret and I take the boat ride.

We hurry to an elevator and take it 'downstairs' to the walkway and to steps leading to the boat. On the way, we are given plastic blue raincoats, and we begin putting them on, which is not easy because we are hurrying to take a place at the end of a line of passengers already waiting to board the boat.

We soon realize that these passengers are Italian. Over twenty-five are in line, and we know we are standing with a tour group coming from Italy.

How amazing!

Their country has just been hit hard by a series of big earthquakes that are continuing. This tour group is in a powerful energy place to help bring ease to their country. Do they know this? No. But, nevertheless, the energy is here that can help, whether or not they know this.

Later, when Margaret is channeling, the spiritual dragon that lives here mentions the Italians.

When we passengers for the Maid of the Mist boat are asked to board, we follow the Italians and walk up steps with them to take viewing places at the boat's railing. Margaret and I choose the side of the boat facing the U.S.A, and this is the same place where we stood last year.

When all passengers are on board, the horn blows and then the boat begins to slowly move away from the dock.

I begin sounding OM and I will continue until the journey has ended. This is my technique for opening to the Higher Worlds that will be with us. And this includes the angels.

We will be sending out positive energy for the entire world of Mother Earth. We want PEACE, LOVE, AND LIGHT to dominate here on this planet that has taken on so much negativity.

Only a couple minutes away from the docking area, we encounter the place where the dragon met us last year. And yes, he is working with us to help Mother Earth.

The water is now blasting in on us as we stand at the railing. Water is a healer. Come on, water, BLAST AWAY!

And it does.

The boat is slowly moving toward the main big falls, and when the captain has put us within this gigantic, powerful falls, the water is BLASTING AWAY AT US FULL FORCE.

GOOD!

I am continuing to sound the OMs full force and I will not stop no matter how powerful the water is blasting away. I know the boat will not go down. I am encouraged by the force.

Usually, the captain puts the boat only a short time in the BLASTING water, but this time the captain is in no rush for us to leave.

GOOD!

I AM SOUNDING THE OMS, SENDING OUT POSITIVE ENERGY.

When we do leave the great blasting water and the captain has turned us around to return to the docking area, I continue sounding the OMs until the boat docks.

WHAT A JOURNEY!

The Italians look happy.

All of us leave the boat and begin taking off our plastic blue raincoats as we are climbing stairs to reach an observation deck. Along the way are containers to dispose of our raincoats.

At the observation deck, I look at the falls, and yes, the view is spectacular, but the boat ride is far superior to anything else.

Now we meet our Canadian friend and two children and we have a fine time with them before we are driven in their car to the Sheraton. Here, we check out of the hotel, retrieve our car from the parking area, and we ask a parking attendant how to avoid taking the Thruway.

He says after leaving the parking lot, we should go straight through a stoplight complex and continue along until reaching a second stoplight complex where we are to turn right onto Main Street. We are to follow Main Street until we reach Route 31, and then we turn right onto that and stay with it to go east all the way.

Well, can we remember all that?

Yes. We had no problems whatsoever.

No half-mile of stalled cars waiting to get onto the Thruway. Little traffic of big trucks on the road we are taking.

Perfect!

From Margaret:

September 1:

It is 8:40 p.m., our first night at Niagara Falls, and there is an amazing fire red sunset. Our room faces west. A red dragon cloud is in the sky.

I comment to the Dragon of the North American continent that the sunset decorated the sky with red flame color outlining soft grey clouds. A long cloud reminded me of a long dragon with uplifted head. It seemed so real. I would like your thoughts.

The Dragon responds: *Margaret, I am here. Much greater than an outline of a cloudbank. I grow larger as the problems here grow larger. There is terrible unease and unrest in the humans now. This agitates me. There are bright ones that shine their Love and Light out to the planet. They are the bridge to the next generation.*

I work for the stabilizing of Mother Earth. She has much to endure with the affront to her being and life forms.

I live on the Land. I live in the Air. I live in the Water. I am mainly connected to the Land, although Air and Water are under my jurisdiction.

High energy lines. Light sounding vibration lines. Song Lines. Master Goi lines. Peace Prayer lines. Dedicated people all over the world. You touch base with many and bring their energy to me. You carry many frequencies in your bag.

I love your love of the 1930's New Orleans Jazz. Dragon Tail Jazz energy. Razzmatazz, syncopation, high-stepping jazz lift your spirits, lift your energy. Music, the goat for the racehorse. Driving music for friends coming across the roads to see me.

It is appreciated. You carry trailers -- Master Goi, Sai Baba, Bawa Muhaiyaddeen, Mary, Christ, Saint Germain.

Sleep now. Sleep.

With my love, the Dragon.

_____

September 2:

3:30 a.m., I wake pondering the importance of the Niagara Falls, the Dragon Guardian, the Golden Dolphins, and the Angelic Realm.

I begin more channeling with the Dolphins. They say:

Place yourself consciously in this amazing Vortex of Power – the rushing water that drains the Great Lakes out into the Atlantic Ocean via the Saint Lawrence River. You are in the energetic focal point of the Niagara Escarpment, the point where all things change -- the rushing of the water --the descent over the rock cliffs – one level to the next level to continue on to reach the great ocean.

Take part in any aspect of this drama. The people come here to feel the power that is the greatest display of natural power they will witness in their lives.

It washes away the negative attachments, illusion of the ego, the little self and allows the shining Self to expand in wonder. If you can feel, comprehend, dive into the consciousness of space.

Allow us, the Dragon Guardian of the North American continent and the Golden Dolphins of Joy to give you a ticket to this amazing opening to consciousness.

Hold onto a branch and hang over the falls with your mind, emotions, spirit, and let the joy of the moving water wash away confusion, doubts, sadness. That is why I, the Dragon, am perched on this point.

Think of the Serpent of Serpent Mound at the point above the water on top of a meteor crater impact area. The Serpent receives, expands the power of Mother Earth. Every inch of the body of the Serpent touches Mother Earth as the Serpent moves and rests atop that cliff.

Niagara Falls sits atop the Mighty Ridge (the Niagara Escarpment) the powerful force field of balance and harmony, universal good, positive energy of the ancient past coming forward to be used today when Light and Love and Peace are needed.

Put aside petty worries of undigested, un-experienced events. All cultures come here to be bathed in the rushing, falling waters – the Power of Niagara Falls – where the negative debris is washed away and the pure Joy of Living is felt. To be honored is to be in such a place. That recognition is the place where I sit.

The place of honor, recognition, expansion into Oneness. At this point, that is where I reside.

Here one takes the highest frequency, highest principles of Life.

Expansion. Creativity. Joy. Love. Harmony. Wonder. Humor.

Soaring principles of Divine and Human interactions and Planetary Grace. All in one moment and the water rushes over the falls to begin a new day, a new life of Joy.

Come let us meet today at the Falls.

The Golden Dragon. The Golden Dolphins. Golden Humanity of true intent of Peace, Joy, and Harmony. Peace, Love and Light. These are all sides of reality.

———————

Barbara and I are ready with enthusiasm to take a taxi this morning to the ticket booth for the Maid of the Mist boat ride. At the ticket booth, our friend Kim and her family from Canada join us. Even though they are not taking the boat this morning, they will watch our ride from above.

A delightful tour group of Italians of all ages are ready to climb aboard with us. They are totally exuberant about the boat ride. Energy, Energy, Energy! We feel the same.

When the gangplank is lowered and we walk aboard, Barbara and I climb the stairs to the upper deck to stand on the left side, port side, closest to the American Falls. The gulls and cormorants are flying above us or sitting on big rocks in the river.

The day is bright and the temperature is just right – not too hot, and not too cold.

The boat horn sounds and we slowly head up the Niagara River to the Falls. Barbara and I begin sounding the OMs continuously. We know we are in the presence of the Dragon. We pass the Cave of the Wind and its energy, continuing to the main Falls on the American side.

Solid water pours over the cliffs. We are moving closer and closer to the Falls. Now we are underneath them. TREMENDOUS WATER POURING, POURING, POURING.

The wind whips off my poncho hood and my head is drenched. I am covered with water. I look up at the Falls with WATER RUSHING DOWN. I turn my back and look across the boat to the Canadian side of the Falls. There is a GRAND RAINBOW on that side! WOW!

The captain keeps pushing the boat against the current and we stay for a very long time in the center of the Vortex of energy of Niagara Falls. Swirling, churning, spraying torrents. WATER, WATER, WATER, WATER.

OM. OM. OM. OM. OM. OM. OM. OM. OM.

The roar of the Falls accepts our OMs.

Barbara opens to the Higher Dimensions and places the sacred moon water in the Falls.

I totally merge with the WATER – the sacred water, the sacred Dragon, the Rainbow. I throw negativity into the turbulence of the water – the negativity of thought, speech and action, to remove it from the continent and the world.

I become totally lost in the FORCE OF NATURE. It is overwhelming.

When the captain returns us to the boat dock, we disembark down the wet stairs. We are all smiles even though everything is wet. My heart is wet and full of JOY.

Now we meet Kim and her family who have photographed us from above while we are on the boat. She shows us a double rainbow. As we are walking with her another rainbow appears! Red, orange, yellow, green, blue, and VIOLET! What a gift!

These are memories I will never forget.

An amazing journey!

That night, the Dragon channels to me:

Your mission was well accomplished. Niagara Falls received the sacred (moon) water and the continuous OMs. The Blessings Chimes were wrapped inside the bag but their joyful healing presence was acknowledged. With the wind and torrents of water, nothing could be brought out on deck.

Barbara brought in Power Positive energies and Margaret, you were releasing negative energies that needed to be removed from the environment -- media, language, thought, speaking. When you stand against a wall of water, nothing stays the same.

The Angels and the Golden Dolphins were overseers. Smiling. The captain kept the boat steady to fulfill your mission.

The kind-hearted, positive Italians, always joyous on an outing, were great boat mates -- releasing the pressure of the earthquakes in middle Italy east of Rome.

Love, Love, Love. Smiles, Smiles.
Families and couples joyous in the ride of a lifetime.

Everyone was breathing water and oxygen!!

Everyone was drenched with the power of water.

A huge Vortex of Love and Joy rose up, framed by rainbows at every turn.

Kim and her family on land photographed the boat with the rainbow approaching.

You watched the rainbow that appeared on the Canadian side. Then you later saw the full rainbow at the rim of the Falls with the full spectrum of color -- with an emphasis on violet.

You and Kim were focusing on the location of ME, my habitat, my command post -- here and in other dimensions.

She is an Earth Guardian of the Falls.

Grace and Movement -- power and awe.

Welcome to Niagara Falls, to the changing of the Vibrational Frequency of the North American continent.

AUM.

==

CHAPTER 7

Onondaga Lake

Joint Journals:

From Barbara:

October 1, the Higher Worlds give us a job for today. We must go to Onondaga Lake to cleanse it. It is near Syracuse, New York State.

Onondaga Lake is regarded as probably the most polluted water in the U.S.A. with tons and tons and tons of poisons such as mercury, dioxins, and industrial wastes deliberately dumped into the water. It is estimated that over 9 million cubic yards of waste are at the bottom of the lake.

Attempts to clean up the waste have been slow and often unsuccessful. The cost of cleaning up the lake is huge.

―――――――――

From Margaret:

Here is my channeling from dear Emma and dear Christ.

I receive: *Pollution is the greatest problem for humanity on earth. Addressing the most polluted lake in the world helps lighten the load of negativity on Earth. Bring Light, Love, and Joy to the lake. Sound the Blessings Chimes to bring Light, Love and Healing to the lake. Putting down the Vortexes changes the Vibrational Frequencies.*

Onondaga is the Lake of Peace with the Tree of Peace where the (Peacemaker) Christ came many years ago. The Peace frequency is here. The people agreed to bury their weapons and live a peaceful life. Let humanity follow this example. Clean up the pollution. The focus needs to be on peace and not war.

Peace is a clean environment. Let all the Vortex energies come out to bring Light to the Lake to ignite the Peace energy within. Spiritual Protection of Nature -- Right Relationship -- Love and Healing -- Change – Growth -- Foresight -- Symmetry, as above, so below.

With love, Emma and Christ.

————————

From Barbara:

For many years, Dutchman Leo van der Vlist has been focusing on the problems of indigenous people, and May 2016, his efforts have helped to bring the Onondaga Lake problem to the United Nations. Since the United Nations uses the Peace Palace at The Hague, The Netherlands, as a location where conflicts can be settled, probably the Peace Palace knows about the problem.

In Chapter 3, we told you Margaret and I attended the annual celebration of the International Day of Peace outside the Peace Palace, and Leo van der Vlist was also there. He read The Fuji Resolution at a fire ceremony, and this Resolution concentrates on the development within all of us of a divine spark that focuses on peace and harmony and love on an equal basis among all of us.

At the International Day of Peace celebration, we did not hear about the poisoning of Onondaga Lake which has come about because of the dumping of industrial poisons. We did not know about the contaminated fish still being eaten by fishermen and by the poor. Those who fish for food in the lake are poisoned.

A few years ago, when we visited this lake to help plant a peace pole, no one spoke about the pollution problem. Attention was on planting a peace pole because it is understood that the Christ had visited here a great many years ago.

The belief is that He came in a stone boat to convince Native American tribes in the area to stop disputing with each other. They listened to him, and at the location of Onondaga Lake, they agreed to bury their spears at the base of a great white pine tree as a gesture of agreeing to be peaceful with each other. This, I think, could be is the source of the common phrase 'bury the hatchet'.

Well, that was a very long time ago. The tree has long since died and another tree was planted. That died and another tree was planted. And another. But, the belief remains that the Christ came to stop disputes and remain always peaceful.

———————————

Now, Margaret and I are returning to Lake Onondaga because we have learned about the lake's water pollution.

What is water? Over 90% of Mother Earth. She/water needs to be cleaned.

The energies of the Christ are at Lake Onondaga. He is a good 'cleaner'. We must bring forward His energies to help the waters on Mother Earth.

In the car with us, we take a photograph of the Christ, a photograph of Archangel Michael, and a photograph of Commander Ashtar. These are 'big guys'. Also, we have the Blessings Chimes and the Vortexes.

When we begin our journey, a sprinkling of rain begins. One hardly needs to use the windshield wipers to keep the windshield clean. But, we drive ten minutes and the rain becomes heavy. VERY HEAVY. Even some noisy hail hits the car roof.

What are we to do? We cannot have heavy, nearly blinding rain accompanying us. There is only one answer. Cancel the journey. Turn back.

Whoever heard of such a thing?!!! Well, we have no choice.

Margaret is driving and she turns off the main road and tries to find a way to turn around. There is much traffic and at first her attempts fail. The wipers are smartly going back and forth and we are trying to see well enough to know how to find a place to turn around.

And yes, we do turn around, and just as we do this, the rain impact lessens.

WHAT?????

Now what should we do? Turn around to do the work at Onondaga Lake?

YES.

The rain suddenly becomes minimal. Who has turned off the faucet???

In any case, we continue on our way to Onondaga Lake and we watch the sky begin to turn from dark to light. Clouds remain throughout our journey, but when the rain stops, it stops for good. Even the sun has peeked its head out from time to time.

As Margaret is driving, I am holding the photographs of the three powerful entities. I am not asking them to stop the rain. My concentration is on the water we will be encountering at Onondaga Lake.

But, their energy is MIGHTY, MIGHTY, MIGHTY POWERFUL ENERGY.

Now we are smartly going along, driving on the New York Thruway, and quite quickly we reach Exit 38 where we turn off the Thruway.

In less than ten minutes, we are at Onondaga Lake Park, Willow Bay Parking Lot. We are here!

We park the car and walk a short way to the sandy beach. Margaret has Blessings Chimes in her hands and Vortexes which she will put down at the water's edge. She also has in her hands two small bottles -- one with sacred moon water and one with Tibetan sand crystals.

As for myself, I have in my hands at my chest the energy for helping to heal the lake -- photographs of the Christ, Archangel Michael, and Commander Ashtar.

Just offshore is a small boat with three males fishing. I am thinking they are probably trying to catch fish for themselves or for their families or for selling. On this extensive lake, I am seeing only two other boats and this is the weekend. Normally, one would expect the lake to have many boats on a weekend. But of course, if people know about the heavy poison in the water, that would be a good reason to stay off it.

The power coming from the three photographs at my chest is HUGE. My heart is pumping rapidly, feeling the effects.

I watch Margaret putting into the water the sacred moon water and sacred Tibetan sand crystals. Then she begins drawing the Vortexes on the sand at the water's edge. When she finishes, she rings the Blessings Chimes.

A seagull arrives, flying low, stopping at the water's edge. Its beak pecks tentatively at the water. Then it takes a tentative, tiny drink. I am watching, knowing that the gull understands that the water is not normal. It pauses and then takes another tiny drink. A pause and then another. And another.

Is this a seagull?
Whatever it is, it seems to understand our attempt to change the water.

Several years ago when we are in Switzerland at the location of Emma Kunz who had lived for a time on the earth as a very high Being, she appeared to us as a long-haired beautiful white cat.

Is this seagull a high Being appearing just now to show us that this high Being knows we are attempting to do something helpful to Mother Earth and all who live on her?

From Margaret:

When I reach the beach, I hold the Chimes and ring and ring them for healing the lake. To help break the negative pollution with sound, I think of Light, Sound and Vibration.

I know the Blessing Chimes are totally in harmony with the lake. I pray for the healing of the water.

For a moment I think I see a fish coming up, looking out. Yes, fish are here. I know fishermen are here. How could industries dump poisonous chemicals into the water, source of nutrients for the area, drinking water for fish, shellfish, birds, animals, and humans?

The frequency of the Blessings Chimes matches the rippling sound and movement of the water.

When I am ready to do the Vortexes, I move to the water's edge and notice the many tiny shells on the shoreline. I am amazed they are here. I did not know there were shellfish here. I begin drawing the Vortexes with a plastic knife and then I change to a weathered stick. It is strong and seems to want to engrave the Vortex Symbols in the sand by the shore close to the water.

I speak and draw the Symbols and Vortexes one by one. When I am finished, a seagull flies overhead down the line of Symbols. He lands and approaches the water to drink, showing us the water has changed.

From Barbara and Margaret:

We have done our work as best we can. Now it is time to leave.

Our return journey is easy and no raindrops fall.

==

CHAPTER 8

Canandaigua

Joint Journals:

From Barbara:

This morning's message from the Higher Worlds is that Margaret and I should go to Canandaigua Lake and especially to the Veterans Hospital which is big, big, big. It is full of military personnel who have experienced both physical and mental damage.

At noon we begin our journey and it is not raining. The clouds are quite thick and some have a moderate darkness to them, but maybe it will not rain.

There are two ways to reach Canandaigua -- via the Thruway or via a road that takes us to the town of Victor and then into the countryside. We decide to take the Victor/countryside road. Well, that turns out to be a mistake. When we reach Victor, we realize the road we want to take is closed to thru traffic. In fact, there is a road sign saying anyone using that road who is not local will be arrested.

What are they talking about?

In any case, we are not local people and so we must take a detour unfamiliar to us. And so, of course we are soon in unfamiliar territory.

We drive along with doubts on our faces, and we turn here and there and here and there.

Then, unexpectedly, we are in the area of Ganondagan, a Native American place which has a big tree we call the Tree of Life. It is fun to sit under this tree, and so we enter Ganondagan and we pause near the big tree, looking at it. YES, we honor this tree, the Tree of Life.

I guess we needed to be detoured in Victor in order to become lost so we would end up honoring the tree at Ganondagan.

––––––––––––

From this place, we know how to proceed to Canandaigua, and we are moving along steadily looking at countryside familiar to us. When we reach the outskirts of Canandaigua, we look to our right, waiting to catch a glimpse of the lake. When we see it, we know we have no more that a five-minute drive before parking at the lake in order to stop and take a good look at the water.

Well, the water looks good. Very good. So different from Onondaga. Its energy is not only good, but one can feel that the lake itself is happy.

Yes, we are satisfied with what we are seeing. We put a bit of moon water in it, plus a few specks of Tibetan sand crystals, and then we are on our way to the Veterans Hospital.

But first we hope to spot from the car a store selling flowers. We have been told to take flowers with us to the hospital. Well, today is Sunday, and few stores are open as we drive along the main city street. We see no indication that any open stores sell flowers.

And so we continue along and we pass the turnoff to the hospital without stopping. We know that just outside the city there is a big flower store and that is where we are headed.

YES. We see flowers!

We park the car and enter the place to speak with a woman at the main desk about buying flowers for the Veterans Hospital. We know she will have a positive answer for us, and she does. She points out a big display of yellow pansies happily growing together in a big garden bowl.

YES. This is just right.

We buy the gorgeous yellow pansies, put them and ourselves in the car and drive to the Veterans Hospital.

Because it is Sunday, we do not expect many will be working, and we are right. Few cars are parked around this huge, huge facility. We park our car in front of the main door and walk up the stairs to enter unlocked doors in order to use the wall phone that we know will connect us with someone in the hospital. A man answers the phone when I call, and at the same time, people appear and Margaret asks if they want flowers. No, they politely respond. They are ready to leave the hospital.

As for me and the telephone, I have no luck. The man who answers tries to connect me to a nurse, but no one picks up the phone to speak with me. The people leaving the hospital tell us to take the flowers to Building 7 or 8 because there will be people who will be able to help us with the flowers.

And so we return to our car and drive to Building 7 where we park. Just as we park, a woman is walking nearby and we ask her if she works at the hospital. Yes. She works at a Call Center.

And then a second woman approaches. And a third. As Margaret and I are explaining that we have flowers for whoever wants them, the women smile with delight as they explain that the flowers will be wonderful to cheer up their dreary room.

Now we understand the function of a Call Center. Its purpose is to prevent suicides being phoned in by agitated military personnel across the world.

YES. HOW PERFECT IT IS TO GIVE THESE WOMEN THE FLOWERS FOR THEIR OFFICE.

Afterward, Margaret and I comment on the work of the Higher Worlds who have to keep us lost so we would not reach these women until they are arriving for their work of preventing suicides.

HOW PERFECT.

――――――

When we leave Canandaigua, it begins to rain. Never mind. Let it rain. We are happy, happy, happy with our day's work.

From Margaret:

October 2:

Barbara says we are to go to Canandaigua Lake and to the Veterans Hospital to take flowers to the patients. It is a bright sunny day when we leave at noon to begin driving south to Victor and Route 444 to reach Canandaigua Lake. However, when we drive into Victor, we realize Route 444 is closed.

We took it earlier to Ganondagan, home of the Senecas, when we attended the opening of the new Seneca Art and Culture Center. Ganondagan has a beautiful standing tall white pine tree that I call the Tree of Peace. I would like to see it again, but a detour takes us away from Rt. 444.

We are now driving on unfamiliar road. When Barbara says to turn right, we actually do not know where it will take us, but after a time, we suddenly reach Ganondagan! There is the sacred tree. We stop to honor it, sending it blessings and love. There it is!

Wow, obviously the Higher Worlds wanted us to come here first before reaching Canandaigua Lake.

Now we drive the old way to the lake and when we reach it, we see many people enjoying themselves. The lake is bright and clear, and the frequencies of Joy, Harmony and Light shine forth. Many birds are here. We stop and give our prayers and blessings.

Our next stop will be the Veterans Hospital and we need to buy flowers before reaching it. It is Sunday and many of the stores in the town are closed. Those that are open do not have flowers. And so we proceed out of town to a flower nursery where we buy a large pot of beautiful yellow pansies. These yellow flowers look so happy. We tell the young attendant that we will give them to the veterans at the hospital and she is pleased.

We turn around and drive to Fort Hill Avenue to reach the Veterans Hospital. Because it is Sunday, few cars are parked here, probably because of few staff and activities today.

We enter the first building to phone Security to tell them we have flowers to give someone, and Security tries calling the nursing staff but receives no answer. Now several staff are approaching us ready to leave the building. They say to go to Buildings 7 or 8 to find someone to give the flowers.

We follow their suggestion, and as we are passing Building 7, we see a woman walking. We call out to her, are you staff? Yes. We have flowers to give someone. She approaches and we ask, where do you work? She says, the Call Center.

Miracle! Miracle!

I have wanted the flowers to go to the Call Center – the Suicide Prevention Hotline Center for all military and veterans around the world.

Now two more Call Center women approach and they are delighted to receive the flowers. One of them says they will brighten their office.

They are happy. We are happy.

We leave and now it begins to rain. I pray for the sun to come out, but it keeps on raining. I drive through it and hear water splashing from the passing cars. When we are near home, the sun begins to appear. IT LIGHTS UP THE WAY!

I thank the Sun. What a gift! The Higher Worlds are with us.

======================================

CHAPTER 9

Energizing Water

Joint Journals:

From Barbara:

David J. Adams has sent information about the importance of meditating for the waters of the world during a particular powerful lunar cycle so that the waters of the world can take on new vibrational frequencies of Light. It is called the Waters of the World Ceremony.*

*See Glossary: Waters of the World Ceremony.

The time period begins 19/20 of July, 2016, and ends August 18, 2016.

The whales and the dolphins will assist us by bringing in energy frequencies from their homeland, Sirius B.

Because our physical body is mainly water, the lunar cycle period will affect our relationship to balance and harmony.

For the meditation, we are asked to collect activated water of that particular lunar cycle so that we can return it to the waters of the world to help with harmony and balance.

To collect water for this powerful meditation time, we go to a sacred place called Mendon Ponds. We call it (lunar cycle) moon water and via the sun, we strengthen it daily.

For healing, we take a small amount of this water to Sodus Point which is part of Lake Ontario of the Great Lakes. Here, we reduce our scope of the world to this particular area. Then we use our minds to make Sodus Point clean as we put in the energized healing water. Next, we use our minds to make all of the Great Lakes clean. Finally, we spread our minds out to the rest of the world.

————————

From Margaret:

Before we leave to go to Sodus Point, I ask Emma to clarify our actions.

Emma responds: *Put yourself into perspective. You are in the midst of a world marine meditation. You are on the Niagara Escarpment.* You are on the Mighty Ridge (Arcturian name for the Niagara Escarpment). You are on the Great Lakes -- the largest fresh water body of water. You are in the force field of the Herkimer Sun Disc. You are in the ancient land of the Senecas and the Iroquois.*

Harmony and balance is the key of the Mighty Ridge. Peace is the balance between heaven and earth. Peace is Equality – goodwill between the peoples and all of Nature.

Go to Sodus Point and express all these realities.

Love, Emma

*See Glossary: Niagara Escarpment.

————————

From Barbara:

Today we are taking to Sodus Point water from the mighty sea that once was part of the North American Continent. Mendon Ponds was water that was once the sea. We take to Sodus Point with us some of the water from that mighty sea. We also take to Sodus Point a small amount of tiny pink crystals that have come from the area of the crashing together of two continents – the Himalayan area. And so we have some ancient water and some ancient crystals. We are connecting the past to the present. All becomes one.

This represents a time period of millions of years. The water has come from Mendon Ponds, once a mighty sea. By using the ancient water and the ancient crystals, we are connecting the past to the present. All become one.

When we first begin our journey to Sodus Point, we stop at Cobbs Hill Reservoir where we often walk. Our purpose is to ask the trees surrounding the big reservoir to send their energy with us today when we go to Sodus Point to do our work.

We have our maps with us to reach the Sodus area. But these maps are not particularly clear. When we reach the Sodus Point area, we need to stop a walker to ask for the proper direction to Sodus Point Park. Hurray! The male walker we have stopped tells us we are nearly at Sodus Point Beach. Turn a quick right and another quick right and then we are there. Hurray! We had no idea we were so close. We had come all this way and not even seen big Lake Ontario.

Now we are at the nearly empty parking lot with a sandy beach in front of us and Lake Ontario beyond that. We park and walk no more than 20 feet to the water and I see the water is very clear.

———————————

From Margaret:

It is very pleasant being here with the broad sparkling water. We are at a beach for swimmers, but it is too early for swimmers. None are here. No lifeguards are here. It is perfect timing to do the work.

I walk barefoot to the water and stand in the gentle waves lapping the shore.

Then I begin ringing the Blessings Chimes for Sodus Point. Then for all of Lake Ontario followed by the Great Lakes of North America, the largest fresh water body on the planet.

With the Blessings Chimes, I am sending Love and Healing for all waters of the world -- oceans, lakes, rivers, streams, water within all humans.

Now I draw the Vortex Symbols on the hard sand near the water just before the small waves come in. I draw 22 Symbols from right to left – moving east toward the Sun. As I draw each Symbol, I speak its name and encircle it for activation.

In particular, special Symbols seem to shine -- Universal Law of Light, Sound and Vibration, Universal Law of Symmetry, Spiritual Law of Equality, Universal Law of Nature, Universal Law of Love, and Spiritual Law of Healing.

Among the Symbols I have put down are glistening beach stones recording the gift. They are the guardians for the lakes, record keepers. What a delight!

AUM.

————————

From Barbara:

A dozen white seagulls stand nearby watching Margaret.

The energies here are marvelous! Clean. I am sending these clean water energies out to all the waters of the world.

When it is time to leave and we are returning to our car, we notice little crystals sparking in the sand. Everything is crystal including sand and we see the shining crystals using the eye of the sun to sparkle at us. We think they like our work.

More from Barbara:

Soon the Higher Worlds ask us to address the water again. We are asked to take a boat ride on the Erie Canal. Why? Canals are open waterways to each other, such as the Atlantic access to the Great Lakes. Canals can help take humanity across Mother Earth.

The Internet helps us find boat rides and we decide the best boat ride is to take one called Sam Patch, located at Pittsford, New York. The first boat for the day will leave at 12 noon, returning at 1:30 p.m.

I phone and ask if there is room enough for two on the 12 noon boat. Yes!

And so we drive to Pittsford, and when we reach the boat area, we need to find the Sam Patch booking office. We stop to inquire at a small store and Margaret runs in to ask. I am sitting in the car waiting for her and I read a sign on the door she has entered – ULURU. What a shock! This is the location of the sacred Sun Disc in Australia. Last May we were in Australia. No one sees that name Uluru in America. Well, what a shock all this is!

Now Margaret comes out of the Uluru door with two women who sell knitting yarns from Australia. When we tell them we know Australia, they are excited to hear more, and they walk us across the street to the place where we can buy tickets to ride the boat called Sam Patch.

Yes, it is wonderful meeting these two women, but now we must put our thoughts on riding a boat on the Erie Canal. We know this waterway links Europe with Western U.S.A. One hundred years ago this link was extremely important because it provided a quick way for European goods to reach Western U.S.A. Now, mainly railroads and fast trucks transport goods.

However, during the building of the Erie Canal there was impressive growth to towns along the way – Rochester was made into a city and then there was Syracuse, Albany, etc.

Of course there was opposition to building the canal. Dewitt Clinton was a politician (US Senator and Governor of NY State) at that time and he wanted the canal. That desire gave the name 'Clinton's Folly' to the canal. Many many immigrants found work building the canal.

We are early for today's journey and so after we buy tickets, we sit on a bench a few feet from the Sam Patch boat. This is a flat-roof small boat with viewing windows. I estimate that no more than sixty people could ride the boat, and when it is time for us to board, there are less than twenty.

As we are waiting to take the trip, we are being entertained by ducks swimming nearby waiting for us to throw food to them. There are about twenty ducks, and there are two large Canadian geese who anchor themselves within this group. But we note that they do not seem interested in food. They act like guardians for the ducks. We even see a group of tiny seven ducklings with a mother duck. Did she have all of them or has she become a mother of abandoned ducklings?

When we board, we sit next to a window listening first to the captain who has a wonderful sense of humor. Then we listen to the captain's mate, another good speaker, who has been a radio announcer. He tells us interesting facts about the canal and especially about the lock we will reach.

What is a lock? I know nothing about locks. I only know that water is forced to rise and fall at locks. When we reach one, the captain's mate shows us its huge doors that are used to open and close to alter water levels. He says some water will rise a great deal, and yes, when we reach the lock, the doors behind us close and our boat begins rising up, up, up as the water rises. We watch the walls of the lock which are damp until they reach the proper water level of the boat to continue our ride. Then the walls are dry.

Now the boat is going a bit until the captain turns the boat around. Soon we are again at the lock, entering it, and the water is going down for us.

What a remarkable event!

And I need to say here, our minds have been linking the Erie Canal with the Mississippi River, the Pacific Ocean, and all the waters of the world.

———————

From Margaret:

Riding on a flat-bottom boat on a highway of water is an amazing feeling. There is a softness to it, a feeling of non-motion except the motion of the boat. The wave, tide, and current motions are not here.

When we enter the lock system, the water slowly fills the locked area and the boat is slowly rising to the next level of the canal route.

The canal is no longer using mules pulling barges as in the old days. Motorized boats carry freight and sleek pleasure boats cruise the canal. The mule towpath has become a pathway for walkers, joggers, bicyclists.

Beautiful trees are close to the canal. Homes along the canal have their own docks with lifts to haul little boats out of the water. The small docks often have chairs for relaxation, and there are plants and flags.

I sit in Sam Patch and merge with the water -- at one with the long passageway across the country. I have the Blessings Chimes and the Vortexes. Barbara has added moon water to the Erie Canal. Now we link our minds to the energized Erie Canal water with all the waters of the world.

From Barbara:

The next day, early in the morning, the Higher Worlds say we must go to the Herkimer Diamond area near the Mohawk River. Why is this area important? We know this is a Sun Disc area, and Sun Disc energy is extremely important for the world. It can increase the energy for Mother Earth.

For years, I have had a Herkimer Diamond. Then, suddenly it disappeared and I cannot find this powerful crystal. Well, today the Higher Worlds tell us to return to the mine.

What is a Herkimer Diamond? A double-terminated quartz crystal estimated to be close to 500 million years old. They were born in a rock and some still reside there. A great many years ago in this area was the Cambrian Sea where the crystals were formed.

Early this morning we begin driving to the Herkimer Diamond Mines near the Mohawk River. When we reach the place, we enter a large building where the crystals are sold. Here I search the crystal display and I find a replacement for the crystal that has disappeared from my house. Also, I buy a small bedrock that has a little opening and this opening shows a tiny gem, a very tiny crystal that was born here and is still here.

At the suggestion of the owner who is a very agreeable person, we go upstairs to a museum. Here we see a dinosaur skull. How amazing!

As we all know, everything on Mother Earth is ascending. Everything includes the past. Today we worked with the past -- millions of years ago, and even the dinosaur. All are one.

Now you will hear from Margaret.

———————————

From Margaret:

When we reach a place called Herkimer Diamond Mines KOA Resort, there is a large open digging place for crystals and a large yellow barn-like building for buying crystals. Inside the building, Barbara, who well knows these crystals, buys.

I continue scanning all the delightful examples of Herkimer Diamonds. First I check the individual crystals and then I check diamonds still in their stone matrix. Some live in individual cavities as if placed there. Others are grown in beds of little crystals all living together.

I remember the Native American story of Manataka where off-world people brought to Mother Earth special crystals and placed them in a deep cave in an area known as the Place of Peace, Manataka (Hot Springs). Could the Herkimer crystals be from off-world and placed on Mother Earth as great healing crystals of peace? Hmmmmmm.

I am attracted to several crystals and I buy them.

Briefly, we visit the museum upstairs to see an example of a crystal bed of growing crystals. Then Barbara and I go outside to watch families ready to dig for crystals. Whatever they find, they can keep.

At the base of a powerful nearby tree, we place a bit of sacred moon water on the ground and sprinkle Tibetan sand crystals. The frequency is so high here, it is hard to keep one's balance.

I ring the Blessings Chimes for all crystals here and for the Sun Disc. Then we link the moon water we have brought here today to the rest of the world.

I bring out the Vortexes and sit on the ground and draw the Symbols, one on top of the other. The main Symbols here are the Universal Law of Free Will and the Spiritual Freedom of Man which form the Vortex of Integrity. Also, the Universal Law of Symmetry and the Spiritual Law of Equality which form the Vortex of Symmetry.

Now, it is time to place sacred water and Himalayan sand crystals into the Mohawk River. We drive to a place at the water that is wide and powerful and lined with beautiful trees. I acknowledge the ancestors of this area, the Native people, and the Herkimer Diamonds.

When we begin returning home, three baby deer in a lush green field along the road are happily eating. It is wonderful to see them!

AUM.

===

Chapter 10

Winter Solstice

Joint Journals:

First from Barbara:

December 2016:

Winter is here. Snow is on the ground. At first, not much is on the ground, but little by little, the amount on the ground increases. Last winter Mother Earth has neglected to snow most of the winter, and so we, up here in the North, we are spoiled. Will Mother Earth neglect us this year?

Probably not.

In any case, it is the beginning of winter and we need to begin thinking about the Winter Solstice. This is when saxophonist, entertainer Paul Winter will give his 37th Annual Winter Solstice Celebration at the Cathedral of Saint John the Divine in New York City.

Every year he sends us notices about his Winter and Summer Solstice celebrations and we go.

His celebration title this year is BRING HOME THE SUN, the title of last year's Winter Solstice event.

Will he dedicate his Solstice celebration to someone?

Probably.

Six months ago, at the Summer Solstice, he dedicated the program to Harambe, a 440-pound gorilla living in the Cincinnati Zoo who was quickly killed when a three-year-old child somehow got into Harambe's cage.

The abrupt demise was a shock to almost everyone, including Paul Winter.

This year's Winter Solstice is dedicated to Sir George Martin who was awarded a knighthood because of his famous work to produce the Beetles' recordings and the work of many artists, among them Gary Brooker as well as Paul Winter. He collaborated with Winter to produce Winter's album ICARUS as well as many other recordings.

Gary Brooker and Paul Winter became good friends, and when Sir George Martin died this year, Booker and Winter decided to collaborate in memory of their dear friend. This would be at the Winter Solstice event at the Cathedral of Saint John the Divine.

––––––––––––

To reach New York City, Margaret and I take the train, about a seven-hour, mostly monotonous ride of leafless trees. This summer, I noticed that the trees seem to have been producing a lot of green leaves, and I have been assuming that a lack of oxygen has automatically stimulated trees into producing more than usual leaves. Am I right that leaves produce oxygen? Well, I think so.

In any case, when Margaret and I take the train to New York City, the trees are there but the leaves have fallen off. It is wintertime.

My train seat is at the window but the big Hudson River is on the other side of the train, and so I cannot see it well. This train is FULL, COMPLETELY FULL. NOT A SINGLE SEAT AVAILABLE FOR ANYONE'S HANDBAG.

When we reach New York City, from the train station we take a metro that goes close to our hotel at 94th Street and Broadway. Once we have checked into the hotel, we put down our bags and walk two minutes to the Manhattan Diner to EAT. We are HUNGRY.

And yes, the Manhattan Diner is, in my opinion, one of the best places to eat in all of New York City. It is not outrageously expensive, and the waiters, mostly male, are attentive and excellent.

_____

The next day:

We are slow moving about this morning, but, when 12 noon plus arrives, we hail a taxi to take us to the Cathedral of Saint John the Divine, which is about a five-minute ride from our hotel.

Paul Winter's performance begins at 2 p.m. and we want to be waiting in line with others to enter the cathedral at 1 p.m. However, we do not want to arrive TOO EARLY to stand in line. It is cold this morning and there is a brisk breeze which makes us feel like we will freeze to death if we wait in line too long. But, we do not have reserved seats in the cathedral, and so we need to beat a great many people who also do not have reserved seats.

We stand in line, shivering, talking with two people waiting beside us who say they have travelled a long way today to reach the cathedral. They are also shivering.

In any case, the cathedral doors open and the line begins to move quite briskly. I think everyone wants to get out of the cold and into the warmth.

And yes, the cathedral is much warmer then the outside line.

We take seats and within minutes all are taken.

Promptly at 2 pm., Paul Winter appears and the program begins with singer Theresa Thomason's fantastic voice beginning the Solstice entertainment that will stimulate all of us throughout the afternoon.

At one point, as mighty music is being played, a great gold Sun Gong is gradually lifted far up to the ceiling of the cathedral, and I am reminded that Paul Winter's theme is BRING BACK THE SUN.

And then a HUGE plastic ball begins slowly, slowly, to rise above the cathedral floor to the top of the ceiling. There is JOY in the cathedral because it is Mother Earth rising. It represents the moment of the Solstice when Mother Earth begins to change course. She begins to reset her seasonal cycle so there is a change in power. The North begins winter and the South begins summer.

When Paul Winter's celebration ends, he gives out a mighty wolf howl, and then he asks the audience to send out mighty wolf howls. I remember the last Solstice when he sent out a mighty wolf howl and he asked the audience to do this. Well, today's audience is ready. Enthusiastically ready. The audience WANTS TO DO THIS.

NEVER HAVE I HEARD such loud WOLF HOWLS.

When Paul Winter's performance ends, Margaret and I know where he will usually stand for a few minutes for those in the audience to greet him. We go there, and yes, he is standing there and we shake hands. He remembers us.

————————

The next day, Sunday, Margaret and I take a metro to reach the Brooklyn Tabernacle to sing with the many, many people gathered there for a 9 a.m. Sunday service.

Because it is Sunday, this is not a good time to use the metro because repair work is done on Sundays. I have been caught before with interrupted normal metro schedules. Well, today we decide to allow two hours to go from 96th Street metro stop to Hoyt metro stop to reach the tabernacle on time. Normally, it would take a half hour or a little more.

At the 96th Street metro stop, we realize the metro lines we want to take are being repaired and we cannot take them. To reach Hoyt, we must go here and there. We obey these instructions, but we do not reach a metro that will take us to Hoyt. We ask riding passengers what to do, and we were given advice, but we still remain 'lost'.

FINALLY, we do arrive at the Hoyt metro station, and we start walking FAST to the tabernacle which was not close.

WILL WE REACH THE TABERNACLE BEFORE THE MORNING SERVICE BEGINS????

Well, as we walk in the street door of the tabernacle, we hear 2,000 loudly singing about LOVE.

A tabernacle assistant rushes us into the singing audience and finds seats for us, and we immediately begin singing LOVE music with the 2,000 voices.

Love -- yes, that will help Mother Earth during her time of struggle for balance and harmony. We sing throughout the whole service.

New York City provides ingredients needed for the December 21 Winter Solstice.

The JOY at the Cathedral of Saint John the Divine.
The powerful LOVE energies coming from the Brooklyn Tabernacle.

We combined these two with the powerful HARMONY AND BALANCE energies coming to the dolphins and whales from their homeland of Sirius B.

The next morning we are on the train again to return home for the December 21 Solstice.

———————

December 21, 2016, 5:44 a.m., the moment of the Winter Solstice, I am seated in meditation, waiting.........

Waiting for what?

Usually I know exactly what work needs to be done at a moment of great importance, but I have received NO information from the Higher Worlds.

Why?

Then, just at the moment of the Solstice, I receive a request from the Higher Worlds..........

Remove those at the African Burial Ground.

WHAT A SURPRISE!!!!

Yes, I know the meaning of this surprise. In the pocket at my seat on the train to New York City, there was a magazine called New York By Rail. I asked the conductor if I could have this magazine and he said yes. On the train, when my eyes were moving from one page to another, page 25 had an announcement about the African Burial Ground where about 15,000 Africans were buried, beginning in the 1600s. Most were slaves.

My immediate reaction was of horror. I thought of the dismay and heartache of hundreds of mothers and fathers in Africa whose kin were kidnapped and brought to America to be slaves.

I remember reading about Kirael who now lives in the 7th dimension but who can still contact the 3rd dimension. It is my understanding that when he last was in the 3th dimension, he was a ship captain. One time he was commanding his ship to go from England to the U.S.A. and he learned there were on his ship kidnapped Africans who were being brought to the U.S.A. to be slaves.

Kirael turned around his ship and landed on the coast of Africa where all the kidnapped Africans were released unharmed.

Today, at the Solstice, my thoughts are directed to the African burial ground in New York City. I connect the buried slaves to the Higher Worlds. A releasing of karma.

From Margaret:

Tomorrow, December 16, Barbara and I are going by train to New York City to attend Paul Winter's Winter Solstice Celebration and the Brooklyn Tabernacle singing. But, just before leaving, we are given a winter weather advisory -- snow. Inches will pile up.

December 16, because we are worried that the train will be cancelled or late because of snow, we phone AMTRAK at 5:00 a.m. and we are told the train will be on time for an 8:36 a.m. departure. At 7:15 a.m., we are at the station sitting in the waiting room. More people come to take the train -- all ages -- families, students, travelers. When we leave, the train is crowded. Everyone is going to New York City laden with heavy suitcases and backpacks.

On the train, Barbara and I sit and watch the land rather than the Hudson River. The train is full and so we have to take any seats we can get.

As we move along, the wind is swirling, picking up blowing snow. The sun is rising and turning the landscape into a silvery white gold. I feel the whole train is encased in magic. The trees are decorated with nourishing sparkling snow -- frozen water crystals. Every branch is outlined and shimmering in the beautiful sunlight. Everything becomes a fairyland as we move along toward New York City.

When we reach our destination, it is 5:00 p.m. and a time for rush hour on the subway which we need to use to reach our hotel. People hold the train doors open, help us with our bags, give us their seats, help us to exit the train. They are very kind.

When we reach our hotel and we are given accommodations, we have a delicious dinner at the nearby Manhattan Diner, a very popular place.

—————————

December 17:

At 1:30 a.m. I am awake and thinking of the need for discordant energies to be changed on Mother Earth. In my imagination, I place discordant energies within a Pyramid of Light and overlay them with the vibrations of Kindness, Compassion, Harmony, Universality, Unity, Joy, Love, and Rejoicing.

The pyramid becomes the Pyramid of Love for the whole world. I feel the rising of solidarity of ONENESS to eliminate fracture and splitting.

Emma of the Higher Worlds tells me to stay on the high ground, to take the high channels and to leave the lower channels to others. I am to live a Christed life -- full of Joy, full of Love. Love is an open highway. Love never ceases. Only sadness and grief can shut it down. I am told to go forth in Joy. This is the Winter Solstice Message from the Higher Worlds.

———————

Barbara and I speak this early morning about the coming Solstice when the energy of Mother Earth climbs. We have been told to go to New York City, a center on this continent where people from many world backgrounds now live. Therefore, New York City has world wide energies – a perfect place to help ascend the energies of the world.

We know that Paul Winter is aware of ascending energies at the Winter Solstice and we will be with him to help.

———————

Mid morning, there is snow, sleet and rain.

At 12:30 p.m. we take a taxi to the Cathedral of Saint John the Divine to be with Paul Winter when he is subtly showing about 2,000 people what is expected for the Winter Solstice -- the ascending of energies.

While riding in the cab, I discover I have an apple, a big apple. I am in New York City, often called the Big Apple. Then I remember the

Goddess Nehalennia of Holland, who, the people believed protected the land and sea people. Her symbol was the apple. The Dutch settled here in the New World in the early 1600's and their capital was New Amsterdam. Perhaps her influence is still here. Who knows? I enjoy thinking about this.

When we arrive at the Cathedral of Saint John the Divine, we must stand in a line waiting outside. It is cold but not snowing. Suddenly, the sun appears and shines brilliantly from a break in the clouds to remind us that these are the special days of the Solstice when the sun is the farthest south on the horizon. The sun's bright surprise blesses the occasion of PAUL WINTER'S 37TH ANNUAL WINTER SOLSTICE CELEBRATION – BRING HOME THE SUN.

We are still standing in line in the cold. The doors are to open at 1:00 p.m. and they do not. At 1:05 p.m., the line begins singing an old jazzy song, *Open the door and let me in.* On the second round of singing, the doors open and we all walk in.

We sit near the south windows and the sun shoots in a big blast of bright sunlight to acknowledge the coming festivities.

At 2:00 p.m., the program begins with Paul Winter playing his soprano sax on a high balcony below a large stained glass window. This is powerful.

Now begins amazing music, singing and dancing, with tributes to past musician friends. Then the music becomes dissonant reflecting the conditions of contemporary life. I am happy when it changes to smoothness reflecting JOY and Harmony.

Now we watch as a brass Sun Gong is raised high to reach the stained glass window of Christ in red robes. With the rising of the Sun Gong, negativity shatters with the powerful strikes of the gong. The music of the organ powerfully reinforces the feeling tone of the change from darkness to light -- with the Paul Winter's motto, BRING HOME THE SUN. I am in tears with emotion.

An exhilarating performance!!

At intermission, people in the audience become friends and share stories of their connection to the cathedral and the tradition of the 37 years of Paul Winter's Winter Solstice performances.

After intermission, the individual artists with Paul Winter are featured. Then there is the raising of the Earth Ball and dancing around the Tree of Sound decorated with bells, gongs and chimes from around the world. This musical tree illustrates the richness of diversity and unity of life on Earth.

Paul Winter's performance concludes with the howling of the wolves. The audience joins in and howls together. It is magnificent!

Afterward, we join Paul Winter in person and he is delighted that we have come.

What a special day! A special tribute to the Sun and to Mother Earth.
————————

December 18:

7:15 a.m., the weather is fifty degrees. We now have to face the New York subway system on weekends with construction delays and confusion of closed subway stops. We are traveling to the Brooklyn Tabernacle to hear fantastic love singing. When we become lost, everyone along the way is helpful.

We arrive at 9:00 a.m. just as the service begins. The place is packed and all are singing powerful songs. Barbara and I join in. Big screens display the words to be sung.

Our hearts and the hearts of all the singers are open with JOY. WE ARE ALL ONE.

When the singing finishes, Pastor Jim Cymbala comes forward and tells the congregation that yesterday a special Christmas performance had to be cancelled due to weather. But people did come, and 1200 gifts were given to the children who came. He said it was a great success.

The pastor speaks of one family he met from Jamaica who had nine children. He invited them to pray with him and he gave presents to each child.

He also told us another pastor found a woman begging on the street because she wanted money to buy her three grandchildren Christmas presents. This pastor told her to come to the Brooklyn Tabernacle and she would be given presents and this was done.

I feel the people here are very loving and they magnetize Christ energy. I send this energy out for healing the world. Love. Love. Love. AUM.

What an amazing trip we have experienced going to New York City, and yet, the exact moment of the Solstice is still to come. The POWER is growing!!

I want to give you a channeling I received concerning the Winter Solstice and the North Pole.

The North Pole is the crown chakra – the energy high point where the energy circulates in and out of our planet. It is an open door, a portal to receive incoming positive energies from the Sun and other planets and Star Systems.

The Winter Solstice is when Mother Earth who has tipped away from the Sun is now returning. It is a time of change, a time of power – where the winter cycle begins in the North and the summer begins in the South. A resetting of the seasonal clocks – orientation. It is a time of intense focus. A birthday of a new cycle. The Earth-focused people attend this great event and send their intense Love and support to the planet at this time of enormous change.

Stability is needed. Many humans are off balance. The Whales and Dolphins are keeping the balance. Do not take everything for granted. This is galactic. All systems living are aware of this event. Yes, there should be celebration. Let us go back to focusing on Mother Earth and her adjusting the angle of her spin so the life on the planet is enhanced.

The Dolphins and Whales are her allies. They keep the focus.

————————

This is from Barbara:

As mentioned earlier, the Dolphins and Whales are receiving powerful energies from their homeland Sirius B to give Mother Earth balance especially in the water which is 90% of this planet. Also mentioned earlier, on December 21, at the Solstice shortly before 5:44 a.m., we begin combining 1. The JOY of the Cathedral of Saint John the Divine. 2. The powerful LOVE energies coming from the 2,000 people singing at the Brooklyn Tabernacle. 3. The powerful HARMONY and BALANCE energies of the Dolphins and Whales.

We combine these energies to help bring a positive change to Mother Earth.

May Peace Prevail On Earth.

Love, Barbara and Margaret

==

GLOSSARY

CHAPTER 1: UNITED ARAB EMIRATES AND INDIA

Vortex Symbols – See extensive information following Glossary.
http://www.starelders.net and http://www.starknowledgeenterprises.com/11-11-symbols/

City Montessori School, Lucknow, India.
http://www.cmseducation.org/home.htm

17th International Conference of Chief Justices of the World.
http://www.cmseducation.org/article51/participants_list.html

CHAPTER 3: THE NETHERLANDS

The Blessings Chimes were created by David J. Adams under the guidance of Saint Germain. He gifted them to Margaret during our visit to Australia. These Chimes are dedicated to healing the world's waters.

David J. Adams websites.
http://www.dolphinempowerment.com/MarineMeditation.htm
http://soundcloud.com/david-j-adams

The Fuji Declaration websites.
http://fujideclaration.org

http://fujideclaration.org/the-fuji-declaration/

Nehalennia, ancient goddess.
http://www.livius.org/articles/religion/nehalennia/
http://paganpages.org/content/tag/nehalennia/

Emma Kuntz, artist, healer who lived in Switzerland (1892-1963). She often channels to Margaret.
https://www.emma-kunz.com/english/emma-kunz/
https://www.emma-kunz.com/english/

CHAPTER 9: ENERGIZING WATER

Waters of the World Ceremony:
https://soundcloud.com/david-j-adams/germain-19th-august-2016

The Niagara Escarpment:
This was formed when there was a mighty sea running hundreds of miles in what is now land in the North American continent. Abundant sea life lived in the water and when they died, their shells joined other shells at the bottom, one on top of the other. Eventually, the accumulation of shells and sediment grew high, very high. When the sea was turned to land, these accumulated shells were very high and still remain. Because the sea life lived during the time when Mother Earth was only within positive energies, the Niagara Escarpment remains with this positive energy. It is very, very powerful. Our book, 2013 And Beyond, Chapters 8 and 9, addresses the Niagara Escarpment.

===

Vortex Symbols

Chief Golden Light Eagle and Grandmother SilverStar have given us valuable information on how to use powerful energy fields to help Mother Earth and all that live on her. This information has come from sacred ceremony and the information is available through:

1. THE SYMBOLS. The Universal Symbols and Laws of Creation: *A Divine Plan by Which One Can Live*, The Heavenly Hosts, The Servants of Creator. 1996 Standing Elk. One Eye Productions.

Original title: MAKA WICAHPI WICOHAN, Universal & Spiritual Laws of Creator. [The 11:11 Symbols Book] By Standing Elk © 1996. One Eye Productions.

2. THE VORTEXES, The Universal Symbols and Laws of Creation: *A Divine Plan by Which One Can Live*, The Heavenly Hosts, The Servants of Creator. Copyright 2013 Revised Edition. All Rights Reserved.

3. The EARTHSTAR WAY 13-Moon Calendar: MAKA WICAHPI WICOHAN WANIYETU, The Universal Symbols and Laws of Creation in Day by Day Living. Guidebook and the wall calendar.

http://www.starelders.net and http://www.starknowledgeenterprises.com/11-11-symbols/

Here is more explanation on the Vortexes and Symbols:

Two Star Law Symbols combined make one Vortex.

The **Vortex of Light, Sound and Vibration** is formed by joining the Symbol of the *Universal Law of Light, Sound and Vibration* with the Symbol of *Spiritual Law of Intuition.*

The **Vortex of Integrity** is formed by the *Universal Law of Free Will* combining with the *Spiritual Freedom of Man.* This is a free will planet and can only operate fully when there is complete spiritual freedom of man. There should be freedom with truth and honesty.

The **Vortex of Symmetry** is formed by combining the *Universal Law of Symmetry* with the *Spiritual Law of Equality.* Symmetry means balance between all things, both spiritual and material. As above, so below. Also, equality between male/female, left/right brain, etc.

The **Vortex of Strength, Health and Happiness** is formed with the combining of the *Universal Law of Movement and Balance* with the *Spiritual Strength, Health and Happiness.* In life one has to be balanced to move forward and also one has to move forward to be balanced. Balance is symmetry in motion. With movement and balance come strength and health and happiness.

The **Vortex of Right Relationship** is produced by combining the *Universal Law of Innocence, Truth and Family* with *Spiritual Protection of Family.* This is also a powerful Vortex of social relationship (based on truth) when the concept has moved from the individual to the group.

The **Vortex of Growth** is formed when the *Universal Law of Change* is combined with the *Spiritual Growth of Man.* Change is a basic tenant of life. With spiritual growth, all things thrive. All things change. Nothing is static. Therefore, both the individual and society need the spiritual growth of man. When humanity grows spiritually, then the Vortex of Growth flourishes. In the natural state, all things grow unhindered.

The **Vortex of True Judgment** is formed by combining the *Universal Law of Judgment* with the *Spiritual Law of Karma*. All actions should be looked at through the eyes of the *Universal Law of Judgment* so that no harm is done and there is no karma. The latter, the consequences of action, can be turned into dharma, teaching. This law applies socially as well as environmentally.

The **Vortex of Perception** is formed by the combining of the *Universal Law of Perception* combined with the *Spiritual Law of Future Sight*. It is important to perceive the impact of one's actions and to use the gift of future sight. Needed now are planetary actions that affect in a good way the lives of the people in relationship to the air, the water, the land, the life on this planet.

The **Vortex of Connection to Life** is formed with the combining of the *Universal Law of Life* with the *Spiritual Law of Choice*. Life is enhanced by correct choices. It is diminished by poor choices. Therefore, choose wisely. Choice and Life are integrally connected.

The **Vortex of True Nature** is formed by the combining of the *Universal Law of Nature* with the *Spiritual Law of Protection*. Nature exists and thrives. It is up to mankind to protect Nature so that all life thrives on this planet.

The **Vortex of Love** is formed by combining the *Universal Law of Love* with the *Spiritual Law of Healing*. One has to have Love to give healing and to receive healing. Love is the greatest healer. People, Nature, all creatures, plants, cells, molecules, atoms, adamantine particles respond to Love. All have a consciousness. Love creates. Love heals. Love is the highest power of all.

———————————

A Vortex is formed at the center of a circle of all Vortexes displayed together. This Vortex is called **Universal Unity and Spiritual Integrity**. All Vortexes bring unity. All Vortexes thrive with integrity. Integrity is the foundation of the Vortexes.

=======================================

Printed in the United States
By Bookmasters